I0181855

Phil and Colleen Livingston/The Naked Apostles
304 Barrington Road
Wauconda, IL 60084
www.nakedapostles.org
email: info@nakedapostles.org

Ordering Information:
Quantity sales. Special discounts are available on quantity purchases by corporations, associations, and others. For details, contact via email or the address above.

revelation of Revelation, *An Urgent Message for the Church* Volume 4: The Main Characters of Revelation/The Naked Apostles, Phil and Colleen Livingston. 2.2
ISBN 978-0-9960102-7-6

revelation of Revelation

AN URGENT MESSAGE FOR THE CHURCH

VOLUME 4
THE MAIN CHARACTERS OF REVELATION

The Second Narrative
of
Revelation

Rev 11:19-16:21

The Naked Apostles
Phil and Colleen Livingston

Published by: The Naked Apostles

WAUCONDA, IL

Table of Contents

This book is dedicated to the Two Witnesses. May their message and lives be a sweet fragrance to those who hear it and hold true to their testimony of Jesus.

Amen

He who overcomes will inherit these things, and I will be his God and he will be My son.

— Revelation 21:7 New American Standard Bible

Introduction to the Main Characters of Revelation

When we behold a person or a set of circumstances it is a three dimensional snapshot of the subject which reveals the moment. In addition, what we see is a result of reflective light. A light source must bring the subject to light by reflecting off the subject to our eyes. However, by virtue of the nature of the source of light by which we can behold, it influences our view of the subject's image because of the qualities of that source of light. Conversely, when God beholds a subject, the vision from His eyes illuminates it. God needs no light source to reflect on the subject—God is light.

NLT Heb 4:13 Nothing in all creation can hide from him. Everything is naked and exposed before his eyes.

In addition, when God beholds a subject it is not just a snapshot of a moment in time. God has four dimensional vision in that He sees from outside of time. His vision sees the subject from its essence to its end. God not only sees from outside of time, He is the One who gave everything its essence, and has granted what its life will serve—its destiny. A visual snapshot from the eyes of God illuminates or reveals the subject from its beginning to its end. Imagine for a moment, a snapshot of a person that does not reveal that person in the moment it was taken, but the entire existence of the person from his beginning to his end, and all that his existence; purposes, influences, sets into motion, propagates and accomplishes. That is exactly what God sees when He beholds a subject. Likewise, that is exactly what we look at when we behold a snapshot or vision given us by God.

It is said that a picture is worth a thousand words. Nothing can be more true than when God gives a vision of a subject or a person. It is not a snapshot of that person or subject in the moment it was taken, but a characterization of the entire existence of the person or subject from his beginning to his end, taken from outside of time. That is exactly why when John is given a vision of the antichrist or Nimrod, that he sees a beast with seven heads with seven crowns and ten horns with ten crowns. In another case, there is a prophetic picture of Jesus that has a rainbow around His head with a scroll in His hand. Or Jesus is seen as a lamb with His throat cut, that has seven horns and seven eyes. Again, a woman clothed with the sun with a crown of twelve stars upon her head. Those snapshots or visions given John are a picture of the entire existence of the person from his beginning to his end, and all that his existence purposes, influences, sets into motion, propagates and accomplishes. All of the elements in the picture/vision of a person reveal about that person something about his destiny, his essence, his accomplishments and the cause and effect of his existence. Visions from the Lord are four dimensional pictures and we must look at them this way when understanding them.

As we begin this second narrative we will find that it is primarily devoted towards giving us a profile of the main characters whose roles in our world have defined our condition and have determined our fate. To have knowledge of these characters is to know the influences who have shaped our world. The Lord gives these profiles of the main characters in such a way and in such an order that the story of humanity, from beginning to end, is told in a linear fashion. More specifically, these profiles of the main characters tell the story from the beginning to the end of God's intervening judgment and redemption. It starts in the Garden after the fall when God decreed His judgment and redemption, declaring that there will be two lines of offspring which will be in hostility, even hatred of each other. Furthermore, that the child of Eve will crush the head of the Devil, his human agent, and their line of offspring. It ends when God's decree has run its course and the influence of the Devil and his line of offspring is finally crushed, thereby beginning the 1,000 year reign of the offspring of Eve and her child.

As we go forward in *Volume 4,* the second narrative, pay close attention how the prophetic history (past, present, and future) of the story of humanity is revealed in a linear fashion through the profiles of the main characters of Revelation. Keep in mind that although this narrative is told in a linear fashion, it is told by giving the profiles of the characters who shape human history, past and future. Each profile given reveals the entire influence each character's life has from its beginning to the end of the world.

Once one character's profile is finished, the next character's profile will start at his beginning and will go through the influence his life has on the world to its end. Therefore, each new profile will often retell the same periods of history (past and future). However, with each profile the story of the second narrative develops and becomes more clear. This second narrative is really about original sin, God's judgment and redemption, the relationship between Eve and the Devil, and how their sin has bound them together. Then about the enmity or antagonism God puts between them in order to carry out His plan of redemption. Finally, we see how the hatred between Eve's line of offspring and that of the Devil's line of offspring develops. All resulting in the Devil striking His heal and the child of Eve crushing his head at the end, the great showdown at Armageddon. Again we will see this story from its beginning to its end, through the antagonistic but binding relationship between Eve and the Devil.

NIV Ge 3:13 Then the LORD God said to the woman, "What is this you have done?" The woman said, "The serpent deceived me, and I ate."

NIV Ge 3:14 So the LORD God said to the serpent, "Because you have done this, "Cursed are you above all the livestock and all the wild animals! You will crawl on your belly and you will eat dust all the days of your life.

NIV Ge 3:15 And I will put enmity between you and the woman, and between your offspring and hers; he will crush your head, and you will strike his heel."

NIV Ge 3:16 To the woman he said, "I will greatly increase your pains in childbearing; with pain you will give birth to children. Your desire will be for your husband, and he will rule over you

CHAPTER 1

The Woman, the Dragon and Their Struggles

WEB Rev 11:19 God's temple that is in heaven was opened, and the ark of the Lord's covenant was seen in his temple. Lightnings, sounds, thunders, <u>an earthquake, and great hail followed</u>.

WEB Rev 12:1 A great sign was seen in heaven: a woman clothed with the sun, and the moon under her feet, and on her head a crown of twelve stars.

"The ark of the Lord's covenant. . ." an ark is a vessel which embodies something. In the earthly temple the ark of the covenant contained the tablets of the covenant (the Ten Commandments), Aaron's rod, and a pot of manna. In heaven, the Son of God is the ark of the covenant. He is the living bread that came down from heaven (Jn 6:51). He is the living rod of Aaron, and He is the fulfillment of the covenant and the Law. Within Jesus, the Son of Man, God's covenant with man is embodied—He is the Living Word and promises of God. Likewise, just as the dead wooden staff of Aaron sprouted buds of flowers then almonds, from Jesus' dead body came life everlasting.

Verse 19 (above) says the Lord's covenant was seen in His temple in heaven which means the Son of God/Son of Man was seen in that heavenly temple. What occasioned this was the cause of the lightnings, sounds, thunders, earthquake, and great hail. That "cause" was Eve's sin with the Devil, the ingesting of the fruit of the knowledge of good and evil. That is why it facilitated the ark of the Lord's covenant (His Son) to become visible. As a result of God's decreed judgment and redemption, that ark of God's words and promises would come to the world.

This narrative starts out with Eve (above) and the Devil (below). The woman clothed with the sun is Eve, the mother of all the living (as is the meaning of her name). The time for this setting is that defining moment in the Garden when the Lord makes His judgment concerning what these two had set in motion by the ingesting of the fruit of the knowledge of good and evil (below).

NIV Ge 3:15 And I will put enmity between you and the woman, and between your offspring and hers; he will crush your head, and you will strike his heel."

The visions John sees in the heavens of the woman clothed with the sun and the serpent with seven heads is the new destiny/purpose given to both of them in order to fulfill God's judgment and redemptive plan. That plan's most important factor is the enmity or hatred that God puts between the woman and the Devil, and between her offspring and his.

This seems like the fitting remedy considering it was Eve's spiritual union with the Devil that resulted in her alienation and division from the Lord, which the ingesting of the fruit of the knowledge of good and evil caused. Again, the vision of the woman clothed with the sun, and the serpent with seven heads was facilitated because of their sin, and a result of the activity in the temple of God (lightnings, sounds, thunders, an earthquake, and great hail). That activity was the reaction from God and the alterations He decreed to save His creation and the relationship He had with man. From that moment on humanity has two new paths to follow, and two different lines of offspring to choose which to be a part of.

As often occurs in Bible prophecy, it may describe a scene or an event but not what happened to facilitate that event. This is a means used to keep the message cryptic, demanding that one searches throughout the Bible in order to understand the message it tells. For example:

NIV Rev 6:9 When he opened the fifth seal, I saw under the altar the souls of those who had been slain because of the word of God and the testimony they had maintained.
NIV Rev 6:10 They called out in a loud voice, "How long, Sovereign Lord, holy and true, until you judge the inhabitants of the earth and avenge our blood?"

NIV Rev 6:11 <u>*Then each of them was given a white robe,*</u> *and they were told to wait a little longer, until the number of their fellow servants and brothers who were to be killed as they had been was completed*

To understand exactly what the fifth seal signifies, you have to ask what occasion would facilitate what is described in those verses above? Under what circumstances would disembodied souls be given white robes (celestial bodies), as stated in verse 11? There is only one set of circumstances that could have taken place for disembodied souls of the dead to finally receive celestial bodies. That is only after Jesus had done His redeeming work on the cross.

The first four seals are about God's judgment of fire being released on the earth, and the fifth seal signifies the release of God's plan of redemption for mankind, whose sentence of doom has already been executed. Nowhere within verses 6:9-11 does it tell us the fifth seal is about Jesus having done His sacrificial work on the cross or that it signifies the redemptive plan has been released. However, knowing what the Bible tells us in other parts we can know what occasioned this event, which is the work of the cross.

Note: This example was only one of other supporting references used to interpret that the fifth seal is about the redemptive work of the cross by Jesus. However, without going into detail, the point was made that in order to interpret a prophetic message, we sometimes have to look harder at what would facilitate or cause an event prophecy may describe, and not try to understand the event itself. For example, it wouldn't pay to try to understand why God would offer clean white robes to a disembodied soul. It would be like offering a brand new pair of shoes to an amputee. You get more meaning out of it when you focus on why God would give them clean white robes and under what circumstances that is possible. The robe is a celestial body and its only possible for them to receive it after Jesus would sacrifice Himself on the cross. The focus, in turn, is not about them getting robes, but about sacrifice of the cross being complete and successful in accomplishing its purpose—to reconcile men with God and give them everlasting life as spiritual beings.

It works the same with the opening verse of this second narrative when it states, "God's temple that is in heaven was opened, and the ark of the Lord's covenant was seen in his temple. Lightnings, sounds, thunders, an earthquake, and great hail followed." For these radical and disturbing responses in heaven to precede a prophetic description of God's ordained destiny, and adversarial relationship between Eve and the Devil, it can only mean one thing. The event which occasioned such a response in heaven was Eve's seduction by the serpent into ingesting into the human spirit the fruit of the knowledge of good and evil—original sin. If one was to tell a story by giving a summary of the main characters who shaped the fate of humanity, then it would only be right to start with that fate changing event that set it all in motion and those who perpetrated it.

In review, an ark is a vessel. The Lord's covenant are the promises, decrees, and (for a lack of a better word) the contracts with man God had and will make (as a result of this event). The covenant or the promises, decrees and contracts are within the ark, or better said are embodied by the ark. That ark in the most holy of holies, that vessel of the promises, decrees, and contracts with man is the Son of God/the Son of Man—Jesus—the child the woman becomes destined to now give birth to (below). The most holy place is the place of God. The ark is seen with God in His holy presence. The ark of the covenant comes from God—in fact He is God, as John tells us. Jesus comes from the Father. He is the answer to the folly Adam and Eve committed with the Devil.

NAS JN 1:1 *In the beginning was the Word, and the Word was with God, and the Word was God.* *NAS JN 1:2* *He was in the beginning with God.*
NAS JN 1:3 *All things came into being through Him, and apart from Him nothing came into being that has come into being.*
NAS JN 1:4 *In Him was life, and the life was the Light of men.*
NAS JN 1:5 *The Light shines in the darkness, and the darkness did not comprehend it.*

The lightnings, sounds, thunders, earthquake, and great hail are the results of man and the earth breaking free and the dividing from God by falling into opposition with Him and what He created. Their sin divided man and the natural world putting them in conflict with God and the heavens. The fact that this part, which is the result of the sin of Eve, is mentioned after the ark is seen in the Temple of heaven, tells us that the God who lives outside of time had made the solution even before the problem existed.

After this disturbance in God's creation and the response from God, we first see Eve as God created her—without defect, and as a picture of the destiny given her by Him. Part of that resulting destiny God ordained is that the Christ would come through and out of her.

WEB Rev 12:2 She was with child. She cried out in pain, laboring to give birth.

Verse 12:2 (above) is the last part of the prophetic picture of the ordained destiny of Eve, the woman clothed with the sun. It is in that child that her role as the mother of all the living is redeemed. In that child, the ark of the covenant in the temple in heaven, comes to the earth in the person of Jesus.

NIV Jn 3:13 No one has ever gone into heaven except the one who came from heaven—the Son of Man.

NIV Jn 6:46 No one has seen the Father except the one who is from God; only he has seen the Father.
NIV Jn 6:47 I tell you the truth, he who believes has everlasting life.
NIV Jn 6:48 I am the bread of life.
NIV Jn 6:49 Your forefathers ate the manna in the desert, yet they died.
NIV Jn 6:50 But here is the bread that comes down from heaven, which a man may eat and not die.
NIV Jn 6:51 <u>I am the living bread that came down from heaven. If anyone eats of this bread, he will live forever. This bread is my flesh, which I will give for the life of the world."</u>

No longer will her legacy of children (the human race) all be doomed for destruction. As she is the mother of all the living, she is the mother of this child of Mary's. This child is the Christ and of the line of offspring of Eve's who will crush the head of him who strikes His heal. All of humanity comes out of her even though she has long since passed. She is the source of all, the human race is her legacy which her life and labor has set into motion and continues propagating.

God is the one who decrees and causes what her legacy will serve. To save humanity, God had to create a line of offspring which is to be set apart, and separated from the line of offspring which is now corrupted by her sin. For God's plan of redemption to be successful, He had to put an enmity between the one line of offspring and the other, because in the end they are all brothers and sisters of the same mother.

NLT Ge 3:14 So the LORD God said to the serpent, "Because you have done this, you will be punished. You are singled out from all the domestic and wild animals of the whole earth to be cursed. You will grovel in the dust as long as you live, crawling along on your belly.
NLT Ge 3:15 From now on, you and the woman will be enemies, and your offspring and her offspring will be enemies. He will crush your head, and you will strike his heel."
NLT Ge 3:16 Then he said to the woman, "You will bear children with intense pain and suffering. And though your desire will be for your husband, he will be your master."

We see exactly what Eve's destiny is by this prophetic picture the Lord gives, which is worth a thousand words. The vision given John is a picture that God sees when beholding her from outside of time encompassing from her essence to the end of what her life propagates. The twelve stars on her head is the crowning pinnacle of all that comes out of her and is set into motion through her life. That crown represents the purpose and destiny God had created her life for. Those twelve stars are the twelve tribes of Israel. As such, Israel can be called the woman clothed with the sun (Eve). Likewise, Eve is seen as the woman who gives birth to the Christ who will crush the head of him who strikes His heal.

Out of the twelve tribes of Israel comes the 144,000, 12,000 from each tribe. Out of the 144,000 comes the Christ, who is the child. Out of that child comes a whole new line of offspring which makes Jesus the second or "last Adam." He is the first born and husband of an entirely new species of humans, celestial humans. Eve is the mother of this new line of offspring because the celestial humans are taken from among the natural humans. The celestial humans are the natural children of Eve who chose to be in union with the Spirit of Jesus.

WEB Rev 12:3 Another sign was seen in heaven. Behold, a great red dragon, having seven heads and ten horns, and on his heads seven crowns.

Next enters in the Devil. Because of their joint participation in original sin, his story can no more be told apart from Eve's than Adam's story can be separated from hers. That is why the Devil is introduced even before the profile of the woman clothed with the sun is completed. Their spiritual (not physical) union, facilitated through original sin, the line of offspring that God refers to as the line of offspring of the Devil. Eve and Adam are the physical mother and father of that line of offspring. After ingesting the fruit of the knowledge of good and evil (the spirit of the Devil), the Devil became the spiritual or spirit father of Adam and Eve, and their children.

NIV Jn 8:42 *Jesus said to them, "If God were your Father, you would love me, for I came from* *God and now am here. I have not come on my own; but he sent me.*

NIV Jn 8:43 *Why is my language not clear to you? Because you are unable to hear what I say.*

NIV Jn 8:44 *You belong to your father, the devil, and you want to carry out your father's desire.* *He was a murderer from the beginning, not holding to the truth, for there is no truth in him.* *When he lies, he speaks his native language, for he is a liar and the father of lies.*

NIV Jn 8:45 *Yet because I tell the truth, you do not believe me!*

NIV Jn 8:46 *Can any of you prove me guilty of sin? If I am telling the truth, why don't you* *believe me?*

NIV Jn 8:47 *He who belongs to God hears what God says. The reason you do not hear is that you* *do not belong to God."*

Above it was pointed out that it was a spiritual union which Adam and Eve made with the Devil in ingesting the knowledge of the fruit of good and evil. It was not a physical union between the Devil and Eve through sex that made the Devil the father of the natural human race (as some believe). The verses before 8:42-47 (below) helps us understand that. The Jews were the natural descendants of Abraham, yet Jesus clarified for them that admittedly they were indeed the physical descendants of Abraham, however, spiritually speaking the Devil was their spiritual father. The Devil became the spirit source that rules their hearts and perception.

NIV Jn 8:33 *They answered him, "We are Abraham's descendants and have never been slaves of* *anyone. How can you say that we shall be set free?"*

NIV Jn 8:34 *Jesus replied, "I tell you the truth, everyone who sins is a slave to sin.*

NIV Jn 8:35 *Now a slave has no permanent place in the family, but a son belongs to it forever.*

NIV Jn 8:36 So if the Son sets you free, you will be free indeed.

NIV Jn 8:37 I know you are Abraham's descendants. Yet you are ready to kill me, because you have no room for my word.

NIV Jn 8:38 I am telling you what I have seen in the Father's presence, and you do what you have heard from your father."

NIV Jn 8:39 "Abraham is our father," they answered. "If you were Abraham's children," said Jesus, "then you would do the things Abraham did.

NIV Jn 8:40 As it is, you are determined to kill me, a man who has told you the truth that I heard from God. Abraham did not do such things.

NIV Jn 8:41 You are doing the things your own father does." "We are not illegitimate children," they protested. "The only Father we have is God himself."

NIV Jn 8:42 Jesus said to them, "If God were your Father, you would love me, for I came from God and now am here. I have not come on my own; but he sent me.

NIV Jn 8:43 Why is my language not clear to you? Because you are unable to hear what I say.

NIV Jn 8:44 You belong to your father, the devil . . .

They cannot understand what Jesus is trying to communicate to them because in the end they are talking about two different subjects. The Jews are superficial in their thinking and are only trying to understand what Jesus says in an outward way—a physical way. They are the physical descendants of Abraham and since Abraham was from God, they believe that automatically means they are from God. Here is the rub, they are talking physical DNA. Jesus is talking about a spiritual condition or spiritual DNA. However, they are not perceiving and understanding from a spiritual point of perspective. Therefore, they are not catching what Jesus is pitching (as the saying goes).

Spirit is a life principle. It is consciousness, or awareness—a sense of self and one's surroundings. It is power or energy causing animation of the body and therefore is inspiration and motivation. It is also perception or attitude and outlook. Additionally, spirit is memory and feelings (not to be confused with emotions of the mind or soul). Feelings and not words are the natural language of spirit. The spirit of the man dictates his point of perspective and outlook the mind perceives through and thinks within.

By its usage in the Bible, perception and point of perspective coupled with experiential knowledge (memory coupled with understanding of a matter), is defined as wisdom. Wisdom is a set of values by which to perceive through. Wisdom is of the spirit and knowledge is of the mind or soul. Wisdom is a spirit perception and understanding of a matter without words, whereas knowledge is of the mind and is a word description and understanding of the same thing.

All these attributes of spirit; inspiration and motivation, attitude and outlook, feelings, perception, perspective and wisdom are all unique to the spirit. For example, the motivation of the spirit of fear is to control. If it perceives things going in a direction it does not want, it feels dread, anxiety, and generally afraid because it is using all its power to bend circumstances and people to their will. The spirit of haughtiness has as its motive to elevate itself above all others. Since it cannot do this by nature and actually be elevated, it finds fault and judges others dimly so as to lower others in esteem until (in the haughty spirit's heart) others are below them, or at most, no better than them. As a final example, the Spirit of God/Christ has the motive to obey the Father and serve Him with all His powers and abilities—to manifest and accomplish the will of God. All spirit perceives (observes), understands, and is effected uniquely according to its inherent motives and outlook.

The mind becomes aware and understands a matter only after the spirit floods the mind with an awareness of it. Thoughts of the mind are framed within its spirit perception attitude, feelings, and point of perspective. Then filled with its unique spirit perception of a matter, the mind can go to work and understand it with words and emotions, then reason and consider it. In the end it matters little how intelligent or knowledgeable a mind/soul might be. Its knowledge and intelligence is always limited by and functions within the perception, feelings and wisdom of the spirit. Together, the spirit and the mind/soul determine the stature of a man—his wisdom and knowledge. This explains why a person who is highly intelligent but unwise will be awkward, hard to get on the same page with like the Jews and Jesus, and totally inappropriate without proper understanding. Nevertheless, man's outlook and attitudes, his perception and point of perspective, his power, inspiration, and motives are from the spirit of the Devil.

In the verse below, God differentiates between a line of offspring of the Devil and a line of offspring of Eve. However, in reality both the line of offspring of Eve's and the line of offspring of the Devil's, Eve is the mother. For she is the mother of all the living. The difference between the two lines of offsprings are which spirit they possess. It is through the "child" she cried out in pain to give birth to (Jesus) that there becomes a line of offspring from Eve that no longer possesses the corrupt spirit of the Devil. It is that line of offspring who through Jesus become as He, is celestial humans with a pure Spirit—not the human spirit mixed with that of the Devil's. As such, God becomes the Father of this line of offspring. Anyone of any descent, race or gender can, through faith in Jesus, become children of God, or they can remain children of the Devil.

Note: By God calling this redeemed line of offspring that of Eve's, tells us that Eve had repented along with Adam. However, it was only after the damage had been done did she repent. Consequently, and not withstanding she repented, only the redeeming work of the Christ could fix the damage.

The vision or the prophetic picture worth a thousand words of the red dragon, John tells us, shows him with seven heads, ten horns and seven crowns. This is a picture of his destiny which was granted and ordained by God as a result of the fall, just as the picture of Eve's was. It must, however, be noted that the prophetic picture of the beast that comes out of the water is strikingly similar to that of the Devil's:

NLT Rev 13:1 And now in my vision I saw a beast rising up out of the sea. It had seven heads and ten horns, with ten crowns on its horns. And written on each head were names that blasphemed God.

They both have seven heads and ten horns. The difference between the two is that the red dragon has seven crowns for the seven heads. And the beast out of the sea has ten crowns for the ten horns.

The reason for this is partially because it is the way the Lord makes His message cryptic, by giving some information in one occasion and other information in a different occasion giving the appearance that they are not related. However, in Daniel we are told we must go back and forth through the Bible in order to piece together a full picture of His message.

Additionally, we can ascertain from these two creatures that through the beast these seven heads with crowns are kings and kingdoms of the same body or from the same single source of God's ordained legacy. This is exactly as the twelve tribes of Israel who came out of a single source, the woman clothed with the sun, and as a result Israel is also called, the woman clothed with the sun. Nebuchadnezzar's dream of the statue made of four different metals and clay affirms it. Although only five of the kings and kingdoms are represented in the statue, it is about the unbroken reign of the seven kings, also known as the seven shepherds of Babylon.

When it comes to the statue only five shepherds/kings are represented: the head of gold was Nebuchadnezzar's neo-Babylonian Empire; the chest and arms of silver was Cyrus the Great's Persian Empire; the belly and thighs of bronze were Alexander the Great's Macedonian Empire; the legs of iron were Caesar Augustus' Roman Empire; and finally the feet of iron mixed with clay are Pope Leo III's Holy Roman Empire AKA: the Roman Catholic Church. The reason only five are mentioned and two are left out is because two had already passed and only the five empires were relevant to king Nebuchadnezzar (whose dream it was).

God obviously had His reason for sharing this prophetic information with Nebuchadnezzar. The important thing to glean out of the dream is that the statue representing five of the empires of the beast was a statue of a single man comprised of five different characteristics of the same body, or five different empires of the same unbroken legacy. That man is the beast, Nimrod, the first shepherd/king of the seven, the creator of the empires, whose legacy they are, and who is destined to be the last and eighth shepherd/king of Babylon. It is the destiny of the beast that what came out of him was to be set in motion and unbroken until he is crushed on the Lord's Holy mountain at the battle of Armageddon.

The reason the prophetic picture of the destiny of the beast differs from the Devil's in that his ten horns have crowns and the Devil's does not is because it is the beast that gives them their power. A power which is meant to serve the beast helping him rule the entire globe when he returns out of the grave.

NIV Rev 17:12 "*The ten horns you saw are ten kings who have not yet received a kingdom, but who for one hour will receive authority as kings along with the beast.*
NIV Rev 17:13 *They have one purpose and will give their power and authority to the beast.*
NIV Rev 17:14 *They will make war against the Lamb, but the Lamb will overcome them because he is Lord of lords and King of kings—and with him will be his called, chosen and faithful followers.*"

The reason the crowns of the seven kings are in the prophetic picture of the destiny of the Devil and not that of the beast is because it is the Devil whom God has given that power to. The Devil in turn grants that power to Nimrod, the beast, the Devil's human agent. The seven heads or faces of the beast, which are seven kings, all serve the Devil.

NIV Rev 13:2 . . . *The dragon gave the beast his power and his throne and great authority.*

Note: When Jesus was fasting for 40 days the Devil offered Him all the kingdoms of the earth.

NIV Mt 4:8 *Again, the devil took him to a very high mountain and showed him all the kingdoms of the world and their splendor.*
NIV Mt 4:9 "*All this I will give you,*" *he said,* "*if you will bow down and worship me.*"
NIV Mt 4:10 *Jesus said to him,* "*Away from me, Satan! For it is written: 'Worship the Lord your God, and serve him only.'*"
NIV Mt 4:11 *Then the devil left him, and angels came and attended him.*

Here is the thing, all the kingdoms of the earth were actually the Devil's to give. God had ordained it! However, God had ordained Nimrod to receive that power and destiny from the Devil. The Devil betrayed Nimrod by offering to Jesus all which was ordained and promised to Nimrod. However, the Devil neglected to tell Jesus that it would only be for 3-1/2 years that He would have total domination of those kingdoms. Of course Jesus already knew this and that it would be Him, Jesus, who would take the world from the Devil and his beast. It was only the Son of God who the Father found worthy to share what would take place in the future and how everything would end. Information Jesus had yet to share with His followers at the time of His fasting. In other words, the Devil didn't know what Jesus already knew. That is because the Father shared it with Jesus only—the One who opened the scroll.

WEB Rev 12:4a His tail drew one third of the stars of the sky, and threw them to the earth.

This is the last part of the prophetic picture of the ordained destiny of the Devil. We have already interpreted the "stars of the sky" as those people on earth whose stature is heavenly because they are the elect. This verse (above) is referring to the time of the tribulation when God has granted that the Devil who gives his power to the beast, can kill 1/3 of the elect in the 3-1/2 year period known as the great tribulation. For the woman clothed with the sun it was giving birth to a child. For the Devil it is killing a third of God's elect—the line of offspring of the woman.

As of 2015 one survey says about 2.6 billion or 1/3 of the world's population of 7.3 billion people are Christian.[1] We will read later in Revelation that there is enough blood of the elect spilled in that 3-1/2 year time period that would create a river 4 to 6 feet deep for more than 200 miles.

WEB Rev 12:4b The dragon stood before the woman who was about to give birth, so that when she gave birth he might devour her child. 5 She gave birth to a son, a male child, who is to rule all the nations with a rod of iron. Her child was caught up to God, and to his throne.

The child is the Christ, Jesus, and the Devil was present to kill Him when He was born. The Dragon standing before the woman about to give birth in an effort to kill Him before He has a chance to grow up is the killing of all the babies in Bethlehem by Herod the Great. Jesus only survived this attempt through God's intervention of giving Joseph a dream, instructing him to take the child and hide in Egypt. It happened as Jeremiah prophesied:

NIV Jer 31:15 This is what the LORD says: "A voice is heard in Ramah, mourning and great weeping, Rachel weeping for her children and refusing to be comforted, because her children are no more."

NIV Jer 31:16 This is what the LORD says: "Restrain your voice from weeping and your eyes from tears, for your work will be rewarded," declares the LORD. "They will return from the land of the enemy.

NIV Jer 31:17 So there is hope for your future," declares the LORD. "Your children will return to their own land.

Rev 12:5b (above) is not talking about the ascension of Christ after He rose from the dead when it says, "Her child was caught up to God, and his throne." After His ascension Jesus remains in the earth to this day by His Spirit, the Holy Spirit. Likewise, Jesus remains in the earth to this day in the body, by those who possess His Spirit and are in union with Him and are called "the body of Christ." This may seem a metaphoric statement to the superficial who think of life only in bodily form, however, to God in heaven who is Spirit, it is literal that Jesus, by His Spirit, is in the earth in body through those in union with Him. It is instead talking about the rapture when the Spirit of God leaves the earth in a global desolation and takes up both the two witness, and the *Church Pure*, the body of Christ in the earth. This is the first occasion in the four narratives which mentions the rapture.

WEB Rev 12:6 The woman fled into the wilderness, where she has a place prepared by God, that there they may nourish her one thousand two hundred sixty days.

The Church is accounted for. Either they are "caught up" or raptured as the *Church Pure* at the onset of the great tribulation, or they, as the *Church Corrupt,* will be doomed to endure it. Whether the individuals in the *Church Corrupt* die during the course of the great tribulation and are raised from the dead in the first resurrection, or if they survive it, together with those who are resurrected, they receive their celestial bodies. Then together they raise up into the sky and join the numbers of those behind Jesus ready to return to the earth.

Verse 12:6 (above) tells us how the Jews and the Israelites are accounted for during the times of the great tribulation. The Jews and the Israelites, represented as the woman clothed with the sun who gave birth to the Christ, flee to the wilderness to a place foreordained by God to protect her for this 3-1/2 year time period (1,260 days). The reason for this is because the Jews and the Israelites had passed up their chance to become the bride of Christ, and too become the celestial humans who reside in the supernatural city, the New Jerusalem while ruling the natural humans of the earth during His 1,000 year reign. This is the meaning of the saying Jesus spoke:

NIV Mt 19:30 But many who are first will be last, and many who are last will be first.

If God's Kingdom of heaven is to come down to the earth, it is to subdue all the enemies of Israel and cause them to serve Israel for 1,000 years. It is important, therefore, that the Jews and Israelites are not genocide and are not made a nation of celestial humans. The natural or mortal Jews and Israelites, according to God's plan, must be protected and remain mortal men in numbers. It is the point of the Kingdom of heaven coming down to the earth to recreate the nation of Israel over all the nations of mortal men on the earth. Therefore, they must survive the great tribulation without their numbers greatly diminished. The woman clothed with the sun and a crown of twelve stars upon her head must be kept out of the reach of the Devil when he sweeps the third of the stars (Christians) out of the sky flinging them down to the earth, the grave.

Amp Mt 24:15 So when you see the appalling sacrilege [the abomination that astonishes and makes desolate], spoken of by the prophet Daniel, standing in the Holy Place—let the reader take notice and ponder and consider and heed [this]

Amp Mt 24:16 Then let those who are in Judea flee to the mountains;

Amp Mt 24:17 Let him who is on the housetop not come down and go into the house to take anything;

Amp Mt 24:18 And let him who is in the field not turn back to get his overcoat.

Amp Mt 24:19 And alas for the women who are pregnant and for those who have nursing babies in those days!

Amp Mt 24:20 Pray that your flight may not be in winter or on a Sabbath.

Amp Mt 24:21 For then there will be great tribulation (affliction, distress, and oppression) such as has not been from the beginning of the world until now—no, and never will be [again].

Notes

[1] Hackett, C. &McClendon, D. (2015) *Christians remain world's largest religious group, but they are declining in Europe.* Retrieved April 2018, from Pew Research Center: http://www.pewresearch.org/fact-tank/2017/04/05/christians-remain-worlds-largest-religious-group-but-they-are-declining-in-europe/

CHAPTER 2

The Dragon Cast Down to the Earth

WEB Rev 12:7a There was war in the sky (the heavens).

Verse 12:6 spoke of the beginning of the great tribulation. Verse 12:7a (above) speaks of the end of the great tribulation.

> *WEB Rev 12:7b Michael and his angels made war on the dragon. The dragon and his angels made war. 8 They didn't prevail, neither was a place found for him any more in heaven. 9 The great dragon was thrown down, the old serpent, he who is called the devil and Satan, the deceiver of the whole world. He was thrown down to the earth, and his angels were thrown down with him.*

The forces of heaven had been silent or inactive for about a half hour (3-1/2 years) in order to give the beast his 42 months of unrestrained rule over the earth. However, God stops the killing of the elect even more abruptly than when it began. In a day, life on planet earth changes so violently and drastically that nothing is ever the same again. Likewise, in a day, the pursuits, purposes, and motives of every single life on earth will change from the chasing after pleasure and success, to survival—staying alive.

The fabric of space and time tears and creates an opening for the earth and its atmosphere to pass into the spiritual realm. In the first stage of this phenomena, the earth only crowns into the spiritual realm causing a third (8 hours) of its 24 hour rotation to face the spiritual realm changing the view of the sky from horizon to horizon for 8 hours a day, to that of a sight of Jesus poised to return to the earth and administer justice. The pleating back of the fabric of space and time creating an opening for the earth to pass into the spiritual realm causes all the celestial bodies in space to quake like shaken jello. The earth likewise quakes and warps devastating the topography so violently mountains are leveled, tsunamis so powerful they wash away islands. It stands to reason that cities are leveled, highways are destroyed, the infrastructure of towns and cities are rendered useless. Transportation, including fuel and food supplies, clean tap water, gas and electric service are all severely damaged and are unavailable. Chaos and riots ensue and life becomes dog eat dog, and survival of the strongest.

In an instant the pleating of space to create an opening causes the distance between the earth and the sun to shorten. This makes the heat of the sun so intense it scorches the earth causing fires to break out everywhere around the globe and the skin of humans to be burnt when exposed to the sun.

A huge meteor John describes as a fireball the size of a mountain top, slams into an ocean. The ships at sea are all lost, the fish die, and it makes the water toxic changing to blood. Earthquakes, meteor showers, and hail pummel the earth. An angel is released who turns the fresh water into blood as it did in the days of Egypt with Moses.

As a result of the earth entering into the spiritual realm, it now begins to interact with celestial creatures. Locust like creatures invade the earth. They sting humans like scorpions causing such intense pain, that the recipient desires only to die.

> WEB Rev 12:10 *I heard a loud voice in heaven, saying, "Now the salvation, the power, and the Kingdom of our God, and the authority of his Christ has come; for the accuser of our brothers has been thrown down, who accuses them before our God day and night.*

Most importantly, the accuser of the brethren who rails against the elect before God as a prosecutor seeking the death penalty is silenced. He and his fallen angels are forced out of heaven, no longer able to be in the presence of God seeking permission to harm and kill the elect. They are tossed down to the earth and they become manifest and people can see their form. In a rage of humiliation they endeavor to punish the inhabits of the earth because of their defeat. However, it is this single event of the Devil being expelled from heaven which prevents anymore of the elect to be killed. As for the ones who were killed or harmed, it says of them:

WEB Rev 12:11 They overcame him (the Devil) because of the Lamb's blood, and because of the word of their testimony. They didn't love their life, even to death. 12a Therefore rejoice, heavens, and you who dwell in them.

It is a time for celebration because the release of these catastrophic events mark the end of the killing of the elect. Those among them who survive and those who were killed that held to their testimony of Christ, did not worship the beast, or accept his mark are said to have overcome the Devil and their time of testing is over. They too will become celestial humans adding to the numbers of those who are the bride of Christ. At the same time, the surviving elect receive a mark from God which protects their lives and prevents these plagues from harming them, just as it was for the Israelites in Egypt who put the blood of the lamb on their door post.

WEB Rev12:12b Woe to the earth and to the sea, because the devil has gone down to you, having great wrath, knowing that he has but a short time."

All this happens suddenly in a day. Life on planet earth is never the same! If that is not enough, the earth eventually slips completely into the spiritual realm out of the natural universe and, as a result, is plunged into total darkness. People on the earth grope around in utter darkness unable to see their own hands in front of their faces. As people try to survive and adjust to these "suddenlies" from God over the next 3-1/2 years, two more life taking woes are released before Jesus heals the earth making it livable, even blissful again.

WEB Rev12:13 When the dragon saw that he was thrown down to the earth, he persecuted the woman who gave birth to the male child. 14 Two wings of the great eagle were given to the woman, that she might fly into the wilderness to her place, so that she might be nourished for a time, and times, and half a time (three and one half years), from the face of the serpent (direct contact).

The Devil can no longer kill the Christians, they have a mark of God. He has been silenced from accusing them before God and cannot have them harmed or killed. As a result, the Devil decides to spend his rage over his humiliation on the Israelites— the woman clothed with the sun who gave birth to the Christ. As he attempts to harm and kill them, the Lord protects the Israelites from the Devil as he did from the beast during the great tribulation. He hides them in the wilderness or the desert just as he did before, during the great tribulation. There are two separate occasions that the Lord provided for the Israelites to be protected by hiding them in the wilderness.

The first occasion during the great tribulation in Rev 12:6 it tells us they fled to the desert and were taken care of for 1,260 days.

The second occasion is after the great tribulation, during the time of God's wrath against the world, and after the Devil is thrown down to the earth and is manifest. On this occasion in Rev 12:14 it tells us the Israelites were given wings to fly out to the desert for a time, times, and a half time. However, during this occasion He is informing us that they will be "out of the serpent's reach." The reason this is added is because the Devil and his angels have been cast down to the earth and are manifest. This was not the case during the great tribulation.

Both of these occasions were for a time period of 3-1/2 years. However, the Lord used two different ways of describing the same amount of time so that we would know He is talking about two different occasions. Again, the Lord must keep the mortals of Israeli descent alive so that He has subjects which are mortal humans, for His Kingdom on earth.

CHAPTER 3

The Beast Out of the Sea

This next profile continues with the line of the offspring of the Devil. Through it we can see the development of that line. As this second narrative continues it now turns towards the third character who has influenced the fate of our world and the human race. It is Nimrod, the beast out of the sea.

The profile of the third character opens with the antagonism between the Devil and the woman in full swing, and it has turned deadly. As the line of the offspring of the Devil develops through the profile of the beast, it shows at the same time how hateful and bent the Devil is to genocide the line of offspring of Eve.

At this point, it really is about the relationship the Devil has with the woman's ordained legacy—the line of offspring of hers leading up to and becoming the twelve tribes of Israel, then from them comes the child (Christ). Right now, however, it is that line of offspring from Seth to Noah and his sons that the Devil desires to eliminate.

> WEB Rev 12:15 *The serpent spewed water out of his mouth after the woman like a river, that he might cause her to be carried away by the stream.*

That would make this torrent of water the Devil spews out, the cause of the flood. Just as the Devil inspired Cain with jealousy to kill his brother Abel as a means to eliminate the other line of offspring (Eve's), the Devil wants to eliminate the balance of her legacy, which is righteous Noah and his sons. This is his opportunity to prevent Eve from giving birth to the twelve tribes, the 144,000 out of them, and finally the child from out of them. Since it is her ordained destiny and legacy to give birth to the "child," Eve has been pregnant with that child, Jesus, since the decree of God's in the Garden when He judged her, Adam, and the Devil. She continues to be pregnant with Him until her destiny and her legacy finally gives birth to Him.

The means the Devil used to eliminate Eve's line of offspring was the great flood. Although the flood was a judgment imposed by God over mankind, we see right here that it was the Devil who executed it, and did so for his own reasons. However, the Devil played right into God's hands serving God's purposes and not his own. In fact the purposes of the Devil in doing so goes unfulfilled, as we will see in verse 12:16 (below).

However, the purposes of God for flooding the earth comes into importance and has everything to do with the second judgment of fire. Accordingly, let us take a closer look at the flood and pre-flood times.

The Pre-Flood World

Amp Ge 6:1 WHEN MEN began to multiply on the face of the land and daughters were born to them,
Amp Ge 6:2 The sons of God (celestial beings/angels) saw that the daughters of men were fair, and they took wives of all they desired and chose.

When it says "took wives" it means just that! If the angels in question saw something they liked they just took it, and had little regard for the women or their families.

Amp Ge 6:3 Then the Lord said, My Spirit shall not forever dwell and strive with man, for he also is flesh; but his days shall yet be 120 years.
Amp Ge 6:4 There were giants on the earth in those days—and also afterward—when the sons of God lived with the daughters of men, and they bore children to them. These were the mighty men who were of old, men of renown.

It is right here (above) we are told that angels (sons of God) mixed celestial DNA with mortal DNA (for a lack of a better way of characterizing their union). The results it tells us, giants! These half-mortal, half-celestial men were powerful/mighty and had their way on the earth. Corrupted as their DNA was and as freakish their bodies became, God still regarded them as men. That is why when God called them all "man", He added "for he also is flesh." Meaning, these hybrids and humans with corrupted DNA, even if they had celestial qualities, they were still mortal men. They are freaks of nature, however, they die to their bodies like all mortal men. Their fathers are immortal angels, and their mother's mortal humans.

The question had been, are they immortal angels or mortal men? As such, God decided and His answer, going by His statement above, was that He embraced them as mortal men. The cultures of the world called them demigods, half-angelic/half-mortal beings, and they were more powerful than normal men. But because they had mortal flesh, God called them " mortal men." Even though the spawn of the original angels who took mortal women were giants and had celestial qualities, they were not immortals, they were not spiritual beings clothed with celestial bodies, but mortal men clothed with mortal bodies.

These giants did as the fathers who spawned them did. They took women at will, and in doing so over time corrupted all human spiritual and physical DNA by the children they spawned. These corrupt genes became embedded into the human DNA. The corrupt genes in human DNA that came from giants would have become less dominant, and through the generations thinned out. This would result in the giants slowly becoming smaller and resembling normal men. Then, not every pregnancy would result in future generations of children who were massive in stature, or born with defects and deformities. Nevertheless, human DNA possessed elements that God did not endow it with. With the right combination of DNA from the mother and father these deformities would manifest in some children. At 11 to 18 feet tall by the time it came to Nimrod and Goliath, they still towered over a normal sized man.

God declared that His Spirit would not contend or wrestle constantly with these corrupted men who were forever acting out of defiance and being lawless. When saying this, He is talking about how each individual man, whether giant or not, in the corruptness of both their physical DNA and their spirit DNA became way too much to deal with. They no longer resembled the Adam and Eve He originally created. Humanity have since become unruly, laws unto themselves, in complete defiance and rebellion to Him. It stopped being a joy and labor of love, but instead a tiresome burden, and constant antagonism with each individual soul. These giants could take what they wanted and force people to do as they willed, using violence to do so—they had no restraints.

Amp Ge 6:5 The Lord saw that the wickedness of man was great in the earth, and that every imagination and intention of all human thinking was only evil continually.

His first measure was to limit the lifespan of a man to 120 years. This was decreased from almost 1,000 years.

Amp Ge 6:6 And the Lord regretted that He had made man on the earth, and He was grieved at heart.
Amp Ge 6:7 So the Lord said, I will destroy, blot out, and wipe away mankind, whom I have created from the face of the ground—not only man, [but] the beasts and the creeping things and the birds of the air—for it grieves Me and makes Me regretful that I have made them.
Amp Ge 6:8 But Noah found grace (favor) in the eyes of the Lord.
Amp Ge 6:9 This is the history of the generations of Noah. Noah was a just and righteous man, blameless in his [evil] generation; Noah walked [in habitual fellowship] with God.
Amp Ge 6:10 And Noah became the father of three sons: Shem, Ham, and Japheth.
Amp Ge 6:11 The earth was depraved and putrid in God's sight, and the land was filled with violence (desecration, infringement, outrage, assault, and lust for power).
Amp Ge 6:12 And God looked upon the world and saw how degenerate, debased, and vicious it was, for all humanity had corrupted their way upon the earth and lost their true direction.

When it says, all humanity had corrupted their way upon the earth, it is not just talking about their behavior, but also their physical DNA and attributes.

Amp Ge 6:13 God said to Noah, I intend to make an end of all flesh, for through men the land is filled with violence; and behold, I will destroy them and the land.
Amp Ge 6:14 Make yourself an ark

We learn from non-cannon rabbinical literature that the DNA of everything in the earth, animal world, and humankind was corrupted at the time before the flood. The Biblical account agrees with that but does not give details. That is why God wanted to destroy all living things in it. There were grotesque monstrous beasts in the animal kingdom created by the mixing of DNA from animals with celestial beings. It was the same for humans. Even humans were mixed with beasts, and thus the legends of centaurs with the upper body of a man and the lower body of a horse, mermaids who were half-human and half-fish, and lions that were half-man. These examples are common ones most people of the western world are familiar with through mythology. However, there are more than a hundred such creatures in recorded mythology. Are some or all of them based on actual accounts? That would be hard to prove and they sound more like fiction which came out of someone's imagination. On the other hand, however, the Bible tells us this had everything to do with why God destroyed both animals and mankind in a global flood. That is, even if the Bible does not get into detail about the corruption of the DNA of both humans, animals, and plants.

There were giants in the land caused by these hybrids. Since their fathers were fallen angels, and because they interacted with mortal men who worshiped them, the angelic fathers of these giants were called gods at the time. Their hybrid offspring were giants, and were called demigods (half-human/half-celestial). They were the sons of the gods. These are the gods and demigods of the world's mythologies, and they are real. Their mythological exploits were romanticized, glamorized, and are made to seem that they are in charge of humanity, out for its welfare. Their stories are indeed false to the truth, however, they themselves are very real, giving witness to what the Bible teaches us.

The gods of mythology are the fallen angels who took mortal women for wives. Their spawn are the demigods of mythology. They were half-celestial, half-mortal men. To the people of the earth these demigods were giants, mighty men who were of old, men of renown (as described in the Bible). However, to God they were simply men, mortal men clothed with flesh who would die like all men. Men whose very nature was corrupted. There is every reason to believe that all the debilitating defects that humans are born with and suffer from are a result of the corrupting of human DNA back then. Likewise, it is the author's contention that the dinosaurs are also a result of celestial and animal DNA being mixed together. This could account for their extinction because none were taken aboard the ark, just as no giants were. They all perished in the flood as God decreed.

In the book of Revelation Jesus identifies the mythological god Zeus, as Satan. A couple of examples of demigods are Achilles or Hercules (who is the son of Satan [Zeus]). The exploits of Hercules are romanticized and legendary. He is thought of as a champion for man. However, being the son of Satan, even having the same destiny, suggests that Hercules is Nimrod, the beast and antichrist.

Nimrod, of who it was recorded about, relied on his own strength believing it was an act of cowardice to depend on God. He was impossible to defeat in battle (recorded in the Bible), and finally it was recorded that he was 2/3 god and 1/3 human. What that meant was that his mother and father (Cush) both had the corrupt genes of a giant, but his grandfather, Ham, did not. Ham had pure genes from Noah, however, his wife had corrupt genes. Multiple mythologies record that Nimrod's mother was also his sister (the daughter of Cush), and this is why his genealogy is thought to be 2/3 god and 1/3 man.

Likewise, it is logically possible that the monstrous size of dinosaurs were because of these perversions of DNA. The DNA of humankind was corrupt beyond repair, and they lived life under the authority and guidance of the fallen angels and giants. That was except for Noah. Things were so corrupted and life on the earth was so violent and out of order that the Lord stated His sorrow for having made man.

NIV Ge 6:1 When men began to increase in number on the earth and daughters were born to them,
NIV Ge 6:2 the sons of God (celestial angels/beings) saw that the daughters of men were beautiful, and they married any of them they chose.
NIV Ge 6:3 Then the LORD said, "My Spirit will not contend with man forever, for he is mortal; his days will be a hundred and twenty years."

That age limit of 120 has been reduced from over 900 years (in some cases), after the fall. Before the fall there was no death. The second measure God took was the flood, to wipe out His corrupted creation.

NIV Ge 6:4 The Nephilim were on the earth in those days—and also afterward—when the sons of God (celestial angels/beings) went to the daughters of men and had children by them. They were the heroes of old, men of renown.

NIV Ge 6:5 *The LORD saw how great man's wickedness on the earth had become, and that every inclination of the thoughts of his heart was only evil all the time.*

NIV Ge 6:6 *The LORD was grieved that he had made man on the earth, and his heart was filled with pain.*

NIV Ge 6:7 *So the LORD said, "I will wipe mankind, whom I have created, from the face of the earth—men and animals, and creatures that move along the ground, and birds of the air—for I am grieved that I have made them."*

NIV Ge 6:8 *But Noah found favor in the eyes of the LORD.*

We see however, that there became hope through Noah. His DNA was not corrupt and he also followed God. He was a product of what God created in the Garden through Adam and Eve. His genes and that of his wife (daughter of Enoch) were both strictly the creation of God.

> *WEB Rev 12:16* *The earth helped the woman, and the earth opened its mouth and swallowed up the river which the dragon spewed out of his mouth.*

The earth opening its mouth and swallowing the river of water which came out of the mouth of the dragon, is the waters receding into oceans. So once again, there would be dry land for the eight on the ark to land and survive.

The basins of the ocean were created through huge shifts in the tectonic plates of the earth's crust. They shifted pulling the continents apart, making the ocean basins an average of 12,000 feet deep, which were the estimated height of the highest mountains over all the earth before that happened—the pre-flood world. After the flood, earthquakes pushed the mountains up as high as 29,000 feet, as well as, created more mountainous regions in order for those basins to have been created. It is a scientific theory that if the mountains were pushed back down to 12,000 feet and the basins of the ocean risen up from 12,000 feet deep, then:

1) The continents would be pushed back so they would once again connect together.

2) The waters of the ocean would rise up and cover the entire earth. This would include covering the mountains by at least 30 feet of water, whose highest peaks would then be 12,000 feet high.

This is important information because John tells us in Revelation that at the end, the oceans reform, the mountains recede, and the continents come back together and the islands disappear through massive earthquakes that the earth has never experienced before in its history.

The geography of the earth will return to its pre-flood condition during the 1,000 year reign of Christ. The post-flood geography of the earth is a curse that caused high winds including hurricanes and tornados, harsh weather: including extreme heat and extreme cold of winter, then rain and snow, earthquakes and volcanoes, desert lands and arctic lands, droughts and floods. These conditions, or this curse, will not be a part of the 1,000 year millennium reign of Christ. Mild weather will once again prevail in the earth.

So the earth truly did help the woman by opening its mouth and swallowing/retaining the waters creating dry land. However, Rev 13:1 tells us the Devil was angry at this turn of events and stood on the shore of that dry land waiting for the eight to land so he could find a way to start over again. Again, what the flood did accomplish was to almost completely wipe out all the corruption the Devil had achieved in the earth when his line of offspring, reaching back to Cain, ruled.

In this case and at this time, it is the eight people who are on the ark who are the earthly remnant of the woman who is clothed with the sun. The Devil waits for this remnant to hit dry land so he can pounce on them in his rage against all who hold to God and not him. The sad paradox for the Devil/Dragon is that the point of the flood was to wipe out the woman clothed with the sun, all who walked righteously before the Lord—those whose physical and spiritual DNA had not been corrupted. They are the line of the offspring of the woman clothed with the sun. As usual, God shows Himself wiser and uses for good, what the Devil meant for evil. Instead of the woman clothed with the sun being destroyed, she was saved by the ark. And all that was evil (the domain of the Devil), it was his line of offspring which was all but destroyed.

Note: It had said in Genesis 6:4 that, "There were giants on the earth in those days— and also afterward." According to the Bible, we know it's true that there existed giants after the flood by the stories of Nimrod and Goliath. The question becomes, how can this be true if they were killed in the flood? We know the genetics of Noah was pure back to Seth. We know Noah's wife, Naamah, was pure because her genetics go back to Seth also, and she was the daughter of Enoch. By this we know that the three sons of Noah were genetically pure.

Next, we also know that Shem, Noah's son, had a genetically pure wife because it was through him that Abraham came, the 12 tribes of Israel, the 144,000 and the Christ. However, there is nothing that says that Japheth, or especially Ham had genetically pure wives. The corrupted genetics, more than likely, survived the flood through the wife of Ham. This is supported by the fact it is his grandson, Nimrod, who is reported to be a giant. Likewise, his son Canaan who occupied the land which goes by his name "Canaan" and the Bible tells us it was a land filled with giants. They were a nation of giants. In fact, the Israelites refused the order of God to go take that land because they were intimidated by their size. As a result of disobeying God, Israel was condemned to wander in the desert for 40 years.

WEB Rev 12:17 The dragon grew angry with the woman, and went away to make war with the rest of her offspring, who keep God's commandments and hold Jesus' testimony.

How humiliating! It is no small wonder the Devil was standing on the shores, angry, waiting for the waters to recede so that he could get right back to work and fix his blunder. It is certain the Devil laughed at Noah and mocked him thinking what good would an ark do you? How much food and fresh water can you carry on it. One year or so of supplies? He was going to watch and see them on the ark tormenting themselves by prolonging the inevitable. However, what God did not tell the Devil was that at just the right time, He was going to give the earth a face lift. In doing so, God created basins for the waters to recede into oceans; which would allow those on the ark to find dry land. God knew the Devil's plan but He did not tell the Devil His plans.

Msg Psalm 46:6b . . . Godless nations rant and rave, kings and kingdoms threaten, but Earth does anything he (God) says.

God not only decides the victor, but even more importantly, He decides what the victory serves. Everyone has experienced a situation when you win the argument or the struggle, and get your way, however, your victory works against you and towards your demise. Adding insult to injury, your victory (in the end) furthers the cause of the opposition—you win, but you lose. Yes, everybody loses sight of the fact that God not only decides the victor, but what the victory and loss serves. This is the only factor which makes it true when it says:

NLT Ro 8:28 *And we know that God causes everything to work together for the good of those who love God and are called according to his purpose for them.*

Meanwhile, the Devil just keeps looking more and more foolish, and therefore grows progressively more frustrated and more enraged.

To recap, there are two opposing forces and two opposing lineages. One is that of the Devil, which had expression through the line of Cain. Through the lineage of Cain, every evil thing came into the world which led to the flood. Including the mixing of supernatural beings with the natural daughters of Cain.

The other lineage is that of the righteous Seth, (one of) the other sons of Adam and Eve. From Seth's line came Enosh, Kenan, Mahalael, Jared, Enoch, Methuselah, Lamech, then Noah. Although many of this line were seduced and stumbled into the ways of Cain, however, Noah, going back to Seth, did not. Nor did his wife. Noah is the father of Shem, Ham, and Japheth and they were genetically pure by birth.

The lineage of Cain is additionally responsible for the corrupting of all but a few in the line of Seth; the line of those of who God saved and who survived the flood. The survival of the flood with these 8 was intended to give the human race and the Lord's future bride a chance to have fulfillment. The post-flood world, starting with the eight who disembarked the ark, was a new beginning! The post-flood world is where the origin of the beast begins. We have gone from the Garden when God made His judgment and decrees where it all started, then the narrative fast forwards to the aftermath of the flood with the 8 survivors.

By this narrative the Lord wants us to know details of the origin of the beast, the Devil's human agent in the world, his line of offspring which the Devil gives his throne and power to. That is why the prophetic picture of the ordained destiny of the Devil and the beast are the same.

NIV Rev 13:2b . . . *The dragon gave the beast his power and his throne and great authority.*

NIV Rev 13:1a *And the dragon stood on the shore of the sea.*

Verse 13:1a (above) is a reference to the Devil waiting on the dry land after the flood waters receded into the ocean basins for the ark to land, so he could start his work over again by trying to corrupt the eight on board.

NIV Rev 13:1b *And I saw a beast coming out of the sea. He had ten horns and seven heads, with ten crowns on his horns, and on each head a blasphemous name.*

"The beast coming out of the sea" has a double meaning. The first meaning is that the beast came from the survivors of the flood. The second is, the sea the beast comes out of is the sea of humanity. From within the human race rises up an individual and empire that is a product of humanity, of its sin, defiance, and rebellion towards God. However, just as the seven heads have multiple meanings and metaphors, so does this prophetic picture of the beast and antichrist—the post-flood line of offspring of the Devil. The beast out of the sea is the seed of Ham and his wife who had corrupt DNA, who came out of the flood on the ark. That seed was finally born a couple generations later. He is Nimrod, the beast.

At this point there are a few things to interpret concerning this prophetic picture worth a thousand words of the beast. We have already noted how the prophetic picture of the ordained destiny God has given the beast, is identical to the ordained destiny of the Devil himself. That makes the beast the human or flesh and blood agent of the Devil.

Next, the seven heads of the beast are the legacy or continuation of what the beast himself puts into motion and establishes with his power. This is not unlike the twelve tribes of Israel who are the legacy and continuation of the woman clothed with the sun. The former case of Nimrod's legacy is the empire of Babylon. It has continued since its inception just a couple generations after the flood and has remained unbroken to this very day and beyond until Jesus destroys it at the battle of Armageddon. The seven heads are the seven different faces of his empire or specifically the seven different kings and kingdoms of Babylon as spoken about in Micah:

NIV Mic 5:5 ... *When the Assyrian invades our land and marches through our fortresses, <u>we will</u>* <u>*raise against him seven shepherds, even eight leaders of men.*</u>

NIV Mic 5:6 *They will rule the land of Assyria with the sword, the land of Nimrod with drawn* *sword. He will deliver us from the Assyrian when he invades our land and marches into our* *borders.*

Although Babylon has endured all of history as an unbroken empire since the aftermath of the flood, God has seen fit to transfer its power from one king and kingdom to another, seven times. However, all seven of those kingdoms are a continuation of what Nimrod perpetuated. This was God's plan from the very beginning and that is why the prophetic picture worth a thousand words of the Devil and the beast showed them as having seven heads. They, all seven, are the kingdoms of the beast, the founder and whose ordained legacy it was to create them. Again, he is Nimrod, grandson of Ham.

Here are those 7/8 kings and kingdoms

1st Nimrod: creator of Babylon and conqueror of Assyria

2nd Puzur-Ashur: the Assyrian Empire: spanning the old Assyrian Empire, middle

Assyrian Empire, Neo-Assyrian Empire
3rd Nebuchadnezzar: the Neo-Babylonian Empire

4th Cyrus the Great: the Persian Empire

5th Alexander the Great: the Macedonian Empire

6th Caesar Augusta: the Roman Empire

7th Pope Leo III: the Catholic Church and the creator of the Holy Roman Empire,

the iron mixed with clay (which is nothing more than an alias for the Roman Catholic Church in the eyes of God)
8th Nimrod: (the first king risen back to life) the global empire to come controlled by

10 states and kings

These are the seven kings or heads of the beast out of the sea that were ordained by God to rule the empirical legacy started by Nimrod while not destroying it. They instead by God's design, successively set it back, impeding the progress of the empire of the beast from attaining utter global domination until the right time. This was achieved by the conquering of the next king and his taking over from the previous.

That right time is when the antichrist (Nimrod, the Assyrian, and the first king) comes up out from the Abyss as the eighth king to destroy the seventh kingdom—the Church. He will then rule the entire world and have his day of battle against the child of the woman clothed with the sun—Jesus—who in turn will come back to the earth in His celestial form for this very occasion.

The ten horns with ten crowns are the ten kings who, in the future and under the risen Nimrod, rule the entire globe. These ten world leaders signify when Nimrod has finally come into the fulfillment of his ordained destiny, which the prophetic picture of him shows us that he will be king of the entire population of the world. It will be after he returns from the dead and comes up out of the Abyss to kill the two witnesses, that he will create a one world government. However, the number ten and its significance, when it comes to the beast and the division of his kingdom and his kings, comes into play on more than a couple of occasions throughout history before the ultimate or end times and global fulfillment of the ten horns.

It is important to remember that original sin corrupted the human spirit. In His goodness God made a new line of offspring with Eve to create a redemption of the human race. In doing so, God uses the other line of offspring who choose not to be reconciled to God as a means to bring that redemption to those who would be reconciled. The relationship the redeemed has with those who choose to be estranged from God is used by God to purify the hearts of the redeemed. Although salvation is a gift and we cannot earn it, we do have certain decisions to make (for Christ). Every bit as important as those decisions is an integrity that we must have when we live out those decisions. It is not for us to simply say yes then go on living the way we always have because we cannot earn salvation. No, in saying "yes" we obligate ourselves to have an integrity to live according to the new Spirit we just said "yes" to and received in our heart. The two are ever present, however, we must, decision by decision, choose which spirit we will perceive from and be moved by— that is the Spirit of God or our inherent sin nature (our corrupted human spirit).

NIV Ro 8:6 The mind of sinful man is death, but the mind controlled by the Spirit is life and peace;

NIV Ro 8:7 the sinful mind is hostile to God. It does not submit to God's law, nor can it do so.

NIV Ro 8:8 Those controlled by the sinful nature cannot please God.

NIV Ro 8:9 <u>You, however, are controlled not by the sinful nature but by the Spirit, if the Spirit of God lives in you.</u> And if anyone does not have the Spirit of Christ, he does not belong to Christ.

NIV Ro 8:12 <u>Therefore, brothers, we have an obligation—but it is not to the sinful nature, to live according to it.</u>

NIV Ro 8:13 For if you live according to the sinful nature, you will die; but if by the Spirit you put to death the misdeeds of the body, you will live,

NIV Ro 8:14 because those who are led by the Spirit of God are sons of God.

NIV Ro 8:15 For you did not receive a spirit that makes you a slave again to fear, but you received the Spirit of sonship. And by him we cry, "Abba, Father."

NIV Ro 8:16 The Spirit himself testifies with our spirit that we are God's children.

NIV Ro 8:17 Now if we are children, then we are heirs—heirs of God and co-heirs with Christ, <u>if indeed we share in his sufferings in order that we may also share in his glory.</u>

When we accept the free gift of salvation, we obligate ourselves to live according to it. That obligation is the integrity that we live out in the face of the unredeemed who rule our world (the line of offspring of the Devil). By doing so, it purifies us and tempers us into single-minded hearts towards God.

This process is called the "tenness" of our relationship with God—God's laws written in the lining of our hearts and our responsibility towards them. That is the Hebrew meaning of ten. Given a Spirit that has the power to obey Him, we obligated ourselves to act out of that Spirit when we welcomed it into our heart by saying "yes." Especially in the face of persecution which will strip us clean of everything that separates us from God.

It is the case that God uses the objects of His wrath (the line of offspring that is of the Devil) to purify the objects of His salvation. As such, the "tenness," or the number ten will be a common thread through the ordained destiny of both the Devil and the beast. The example above shows us how the ten horns apply to the end times and global fulfillment of prophecy. We will see in the following how the ten horns are fulfilled during the contemporary and regional expression of the beast as described in Daniel.

We must continually keep in mind these visions are prophetic pictures of real individual characters in history who have influenced the fate of the world. This beast is a person. Why then is he depicted as a beast? He starts out as a man who lives and dies. However, part of his ordained destiny is to come back from among the dead, a disembodied soul clothed again with flesh. That in itself is not significant, because on the last day the Lord will call all of humanity out of the grave in their disembodied state and reclothe them with a body in order to face judgment.

However, what makes Nimrod's return significant is the fact that it is not the Lord who gives him a body. Nimrod comes back from the dead and inhabits a body made by human hands, specifically by the false prophet. He is called a soulless "beast" by God at this point. Jesus refers to him when he is risen in this body created by human hands, as an "abomination" of nature—a freak. "The abomination which causes desolation," even, "the desolator." The creation of a body for him to escape the Abyss in Hades is such an affront or abomination to God that He withdraws His Spirit from the earth. In fact, it is exactly these types of endeavors that caused God to bring on the flood.

God gives the world over to what the whole world wants, for that abomination of nature to be king over them and protect them from God. The Bible doesn't even refer to the body that is crafted for him to inhabit as a "body" or his body/person, but as the "image of the beast." As such, many mistakenly assume the Bible is talking about a statue of the beast or some such thing. It says:

NIV Rev 13:15 *He (the false prophet) was given <u>power to give breath to the image of the first beast</u>, so that it could speak and cause all who refused to worship the image to be killed.*

That image is the body the false prophet fashioned for him to inhabit.

> WEB Rev 13:2 *The beast which I saw was like a leopard, and his feet were like those of a bear, and his mouth like the mouth of a lion. <u>The dragon gave him his power, his throne, and great authority.</u>*

We must remember what John sees is a prophetic picture or characterization of the individual that it is speaking of—the beast and not the true form of his body. The body of the beast which depicts his ordained destiny is like a leopard, feet of a bear, and mouth of a lion. In Daniel's vision it depicts the Babylonian Empire as a lion, the Mede-Persian Empire as a bear, the Greek Empire as a leopard, and the Roman Empire as a terrifying beast that defies description. It is interesting that the body of the beast is like a leopard because the western world had adapted Greek culture, religion, and thinking. Even the Greek language was the second language of choice in the world. This is due to a plan that Alexander the Great carried out which was called, "hellenization." It was done to promote his empire's longevity. However, it did predispose the western world into Greek thinking. This is why the body of the beast is like the leopard, the western world takes its identity in Greek culture.

WEB Rev 13:3a One of his heads looked like it had been wounded fatally. His fatal wound was healed
..

This has a double manifestation. The fatal head wound was given to the Roman Empire when Rome (the head of the empire) was sacked more than once. Rome had no real government and the empire was divided up and ten different horns or kings who carved up the empire forming ten different nations from it. Pope Leo III, the little horn with eyes and a boastful mouth, also ruled as a king. He was sovereign over the papal states which was comprised of central Italy, the city Rome, and other small territories to the north and south of central Italy. He revived the Roman Empire who had received a fatal head wound by the sacking of Rome. Pope Leo III raised it back to power creating what was eventually to be called, the Holy Roman Empire. "Holy" because by design the seat of the pope became the authority over the emperor of the newly revived empire as well as over the balance of the kings and nations which comprised it. Finally, the legs of iron have become the feet of clay mixed with iron with its ten toes. Daniel's prophecy tells it all perfectly before it happened:

NAS DA 7:1 In the first year of Belshazzar king of Babylon Daniel saw a dream and visions in his mind as he lay on his bed; then he wrote the dream down and related the following summary of it.
NAS DA 7:2 Daniel said, "I was looking in my vision by night, and behold, the four winds of heaven were stirring up the great sea.
NAS DA 7:3 "And four great beasts were coming up from the sea, different from one another.

The four winds of heaven stirring up the sea are the four winds of God's destruction released as the first four seals. The sea which is stirred up is the sea of humanity. The four great beasts Daniel saw are four of the remaining seven kings and kingdoms of the beast going forward in history. They are the legacy of the beast who came out of the sea. They are:

1) The lion: Nebuchadnezzar: the Neo-Babylonian Empire
2) The bear: Cyrus the Great, the Medo-Persian Empire
3) The leopard: Alexander the Great, the Macedonian Empire
4) The dreadful beast with iron teeth: Caesar Augusta, the Roman Empire

NAS DA 7:4 *"The first was like a lion and had the wings of an eagle. I kept looking until its wings were plucked, and it was lifted up from the ground and made to stand on two feet like a man; a human mind also was given to it.*

The lion was the mascot of Babylon. It was believed that (in keeping with Nimrod) a king of Babylon had to hunt and kill a lion to show his worth as a king. The wings of an eagle, represents the swiftness of Nebuchadnezzar's Babylonian Army which could swoop down upon its prey and whisk it away. This lion as ferocious a predator as Nebuchadnezzar was, it tells us that God plucked his wings and he was lifted up on two feet like a human and was given a human mind, perhaps compassion is what was included. This is referring to Nebuchadnezzar losing his mind and living like a beast and eating grass for seven years as a means of God to humble him (Da 4:28-37).

NAS DA 7:5 *"And behold, another beast, a second one, resembling a bear. And it was raised up on one side, and three ribs were in its mouth between its teeth; and thus they said to it, 'Arise, devour much meat!'*

The Medo-Persian Empire was known as like a bear in that by sheer force of strength (numbers) it would devour its enemies. It having raised up on one side is the Persians becoming the dominant force of the alliance and eventual head. God was giving it power and leave to rise up and conquer—devour much meat. The three ribs in its mouth represented them having devoured Lydia, Babylon, and Egypt.

NAS DA 7:6 "*After this I kept looking, and behold, another one, like a leopard, which had on its back four wings of a bird; the beast also had four heads, and dominion was given to it.*"

Alexander the Great did not rely on shear force and numbers, but was smaller, sleeker, faster, and smarter about conquering his prey. The four wings on the back of the leopard represents his four generals who eventually took over his kingdom dividing it four ways after Alexander died. The wings represented how swiftly Alexander's army would travel and conquer the world.

NAS DA 7:7 "*After this I kept looking in the night visions, and behold, a fourth beast, dreadful and terrifying and extremely strong; and it had large iron teeth. It devoured and crushed and trampled down the remainder with its feet; and it was different from all the beasts that were before it, and it had ten horns.*"

It is like the statue in Nebuchadnezzar's dream. It consists of four empires. However, it must be noted that those four empires together are the statue of one man. That man is whose life and legacy those four beasts and all the empires associated with the seven heads of the beast come out of, or are a result of.

It is the same for anyone of those seven kings/heads. The sixth king and kingdom or head of the beast, for example, is Caesar Augusta: the Roman Empire. After he died there were more than a hundred emperors that sat in his seat after him, the seat of power that he created. However, even though he died and others ruled his legacy, what he established and set into motion God sees them all as him—the sixth king. That is the case until what Caesar Augusta established and set into motion is broken and brought to an end. In that case, it would be the next in line of the seven kings.

As long as what the beast out of the water established and set into motion continues unbroken or is not brought to an end, all seven heads and horns and kingdoms are his legacy and can be identified as him, what has come out of him. But what comes out of him (his horns and different heads) are not him, meaning, they are not the whole of him but appendages of his, or the fruit of what he is and what comes out of him. He is the whole statue, the sum total of its parts, not one of its parts. With this in mind let us look at the fourth beast.

The fourth beast is the Roman Empire. It is one of the faces (or one of the heads) of the beast who came out of the sea. The ten horns (above) reflect the later part of the prophetic picture of the beast. These horns (as all prophecy) have a contemporary and regional expression/meaning, and also an end times and global expression/meaning.

NAS DA 7:8 *"While I was contemplating the horns, behold, another horn, a little one, came up among them, and three of the first horns were pulled out by the roots before it; and behold, this horn possessed eyes like the eyes of a man and a mouth uttering great boasts.*

The Roman Empire does not come to an end like the five previous empires in that it is overrun and absorbed by the king who conquered it. Instead, it is kind of picked apart or metamorphizes into a different form after being revived. In reality, the ten kingdoms who conquered it formed a confederation of sorts, instituted and led by the pope in Rome which, in effect, revived the fallen empire with its conquerors under the pope as its new leaders. The pope in Rome was the central power and authority for this revived Roman Empire, now known as the Holy Roman Empire. As such, and because the pope and his Papal States were headquartered in Rome, Rome remains the great city, Babylon, who rules the kings of the world.

The Roman Empire had already divided into two empires; the Eastern Roman Empire and the Western Roman Empire. The Western being the Roman Empire centered in Rome, from which the Empire has its origin as a legacy of Caesar Augusta, the creator of the Roman Empire. The Eastern being the Byzantine Empire centered in Constantinople, which continued for a 1,000 years more that the Western Empire did (in its original glory). The Byzantine Empire finally gave way to the Ottoman Empire (a Muslim Empire).

However, the focus is Rome, which continues to be, the great city, or the center of Babylon. The Western Roman Empire became a confederation of ten toes, the ten nations who conquered it and was gathered under the authority of the pope in Rome. That is the same ten nations who conquered the Roman Empire.

There are three major different schools of thought of who those ten kingdoms were at that time. All three do not disagree in any major way. According to Mede, those ten kingdoms are:

- Saxons
- Suevians and Alans
- Greeks
- Britons (Great Britain)
- Burgundians
- Franks
- Ostrogoths
- Almanes
- Visigoths
- Vandals

This is in keeping with Nebuchadnezzar's dream of the statue which represented the last five empires of the beast—the man the statue was of—Nimrod. According to the statue, the Roman Empire which were two legs of iron (the Western and Eastern Empires) gave way from iron to be a mixture of clay and iron on the feet; which had ten toes. The statue tells us the Roman Empire metamorphizes into a differ form rather than having been defeated by being conquered and destroyed by the next kingdom. The ten horns of the Roman Empire are exactly like the other vision of Daniel's, the ram with two horns (the Persian's and the Medes—the Persian Empire) and the goat with a single horn between its eyes (Alexander the Great's Empire):

NIV Da 8:7 *I saw him attack the ram furiously, striking the ram and shattering his two horns. The ram was powerless to stand against him; the goat knocked him to the ground and trampled on him, and none could rescue the ram from his power.*
NIV Da 8:8 *The goat became very great, but at the height of his power his large horn was broken off, and in its place four prominent horns grew up toward the four winds of heaven.*

NIV Da 8:20 *The two-horned ram that you saw represents the kings of Media and Persia.*
NIV Da 8:21 *The shaggy goat is the king of Greece, and the large horn between his eyes is the first king.*
NIV Da 8:22 *The four horns that replaced the one that was broken off represent four kingdoms that will emerge from his nation but will not have the same power.*

The single horn (Alexander) which was broken off was the death of Alexander. However, it was not the end of the goat—the empire he created. The goat or empire remained and in its place four other horns (powers or kingdoms) grew up. After the death of Alexander, his four top generals divided up his empire into four different states or kingdoms. However, the four kingdoms were the legacy of the same empire which was the creation of Alexander. The four kingdoms or states continued to be known as the Greek Empire.

In the case of the fourth beast (the Roman Empire), it had ten horns. It was to divide up into ten kingdoms collectively being the Roman Empire in its metamorphized form. That became the case. During the fifth-century the Roman Empire were defeated by ten different kings and kingdoms (the ten horns). The Roman Church, and its popes kept Rome, the city, from being destroyed by them dealing with the Germanic tribes which sacked it. They had let the church of Rome remain intact. This left a void of power in Rome itself and its surrounding territories.

After the Roman Empire fell, the Roman Catholic Church and, more specifically, the popes of it became more and more involved with managing the secular government of Rome and its surrounding territories. In this void, the pope became a temporal power over Rome supported by the other kings who ruled the lands of the Roman Empire during the sixth and seventh century. Through gifts and grants, the seat of the pope gradually accumulated a great deal of central Italy as his own lands. One of the major gifts of land was given by "Peter's Patrimony." Pepin's donation was made 755 AD, and was confirmed and enlarged by Charlemagne (his son), 774 AD. The pope had now become a bishop-king. He ruled the believers as their pope, the Vicar of Christ, and also as the king or ruler of a lion share of Italy.

With this development the little horn with eyes of a man and a boastful mouth arose among the ten. That little horn is the pope of the Catholic Church. The eyes like a human depict spiritual sight, to be a prophet or to know and understand the prophets of God. It's interesting that the seat of the pope over the church is called (in English) "the Holy See." That little horn is the pope and his seat of Holy See (over the Roman Catholic Church). It was a "little" horn because the territory the pope was secular king over was substantial but not nearly as big as the territories of the ten horns. As for the boastful mouth, in Revelation its says.

NIV Rev 18:7 . . . *In her heart she boasts, 'I sit as queen; I am not a widow, and I will never mourn.'*

It was around this time that because of the secular kingdom of the pope and Roman Church, that three of the other kingdoms were uprooted. They came against the church and its claim to its territories, known now as the Papal States. Their efforts resulted in the loss of their territories and their place in history. Those three of the ten horns are:
1) The Vandals
2) The Ostrogoths
3) The Lombards (The Suevians).

They all have disappeared from history, nothing remains of them. Note: Again, there is some minor dispute over the identity of these three kingdoms.

The Papal States included Rome. These lands the pope was king of started around 754 AD until 1870 AD. It was just before the turn of the century in the late 700's that Pope Leo III was assaulted on the streets of Rome causing him to withdraw to France for protection given by Charlemagne, the king of the Franks. Charlemagne not only protected him but intervened by negotiating with Leo's rivals and restoring him to his position as pope and king of the Papal States.

As a result of the attack on him and his need to flee seeking protection, Leo realized that he needed power behind his authority to enforce it. On Christmas Day December 25, 800 AD when Charlemagne was present at a Christmas service, praying at the altar of St Peter's Basilica in Rome. At which time Pope Leo III came up from behind him and lowered a crown upon his head making him emperor of the Roman Empire. This caught Charlemagne completely by surprise. The Christmas service turned into a coronation making Charlemagne emperor of the Roman Empire. Although he accepted the crown, it was recorded that he was disillusioned and angry. He realized that since Pope Leo chose him and put the crown on his head, it made Pope Leo an authority over him. From then forward the pope was an authority above the emperor and the kings of the newly revived (Holy) Roman Empire.

Note: It was not actually referred to as the "Holy Roman Empire" until sometime later. Nevertheless, the pope of the Roman Catholic Church, the little horn with eyes like a human being, the authority over the other horns or kings of the Roman Empire is how this revived Roman Empire shaped up taking on a different shape— the head wound healed (Rome). One other thing distinguishes it from the former Roman Empire. It was on that fateful Christmas Day that the pope became the seventh shepherd/king of Babylon, and began the seventh kingdom of the beast—the seventh head (of the beast), which has remained unbroken and remains the seventh kingdom of the beast to this day.

Note: As the Italian people desired to form their broken state into a self-ruled nation, it fought the pope and took the Papal States by force of arms making them a part of the nation of Italy. Likewise, it desired for Rome to be its capitol. By force, in 1870 the Papal States and Rome were taken to be part of the nation of Italy. The pope, Pius IX withdrew into the Vatican and was prisoner there because the nation Italy thought better than to storm the Vatican. Therefore, the Vatican City was all the territory left of the Papal States in which the pope is king over. Pius IX and the succeeding popes refused to recognize Italy as a nation, and they held out, unable to leave the Vatican. They were unwilling to let it come under the sovereignty of the nation of Italy.

In 1920, Benito Mussolini, the fascist dictator of Italy who became an alley of Hitler's in World War II, made the Lateran Treaty with the Roman Church. He recognized the Vatican City as the Roman Catholic Church's own city-state to be self-ruled, and no longer sought to absorb it into the nation of Italy. The great standoff was finally resolved. He also gave a great deal of finances. This is important because as a result, the Roman Catholic Church remained a sovereign state. The pope to this day is a bishop-king; bishop of the Roman Catholic Church, the Holy See, and king, sovereign ruler of the city-state, the Vatican. In return and according to the stipulations of the treaty, the pope and his church finally acknowledged Italy as a nation.

NAS JN 18:36 Jesus answered, "My kingdom is not of this world. If My kingdom were of this world, then My servants would be fighting so that I would not be handed over to the Jews; but as it is, My kingdom is not of this realm."

It was a metamorphosis or transition which happened over time that the papacy became the seventh king and kingdom of the beast:

- From the time of Emperor Constantine the church began to partnership with the Roman Empire, leaning on the Roman emperor and working with him for power, protection, stature, while receiving riches, properties, and buildings.

- When Rome fell, the papacy of the Roman Church capitalized on the void of power and became a sovereign king over the territories of the papal states (central Italy including, Rome itself).

- Then in an attempt to empower itself, the papacy revived the Roman Empire by stepping into that authority by crowning the king of France the emperor of the Roman Empire. This was the head of the beast which received a fatal blow but was revived.

- The pope becoming a secular sovereign over territories including Rome and central Italy, then finally revived the Roman Empire in 800 AD while putting himself and the church in authority over it. It became the iron mixed with clay, and the ten toes confederation which (originally) made up the Holy Roman Empire.

If this were not enough, it is important to note that the papacy is one of the few remaining sovereignties in the world today. The pope is still an absolute monarch even though his kingdom is the smallest sovereignty (Vatican City), with the smallest national population. It is the only national state which can qualify as being the continuation of the Roman Empire as a result of it being an absolute monarch.

The papacy is the seventh king of the seventh kingdom of the beast. The little horn, the papacy, is not the beast or the antichrist. The beast, the individual named Nimrod, is not one of the horns on his own head. Neither is he the beast of Daniel with iron jaws. That beast in Daniel is one of the seven heads of the beast who came out of the water—it is an appendage of the beast. All the heads and all the beasts of Daniel and their horns together are the individual, Nimrod, who is the beast out of the water. When he returns as the eighth king, he will destroy the seventh kingdom—the church and prostitute.

The second expression of the fatal head wound being healed is the person Nimrod himself—the beast out of the sea. Antiquity holds that Nimrod died of a head wound. Some sources say it was decapitation. We learn in both Daniel and here in Revelation that it is the false prophet who will create a body and call the beast/Nimrod up out of the Abyss to be clothed in it. Then the beast, Nimrod, will once again be among us, the living, and finally fulfill his ordained destiny as ruler of the entire world. It is interesting to note that both his empirical legacy, the Roman Empire, and his person are healed and revived from a deathblow to the head by the same source. That is the little horn—the pope, the Holy See, the false prophet, and finally king of the seventh kingdom. It was a pope who healed the head wound of the empire and it will be a pope and seventh king who will revive the beast, Nimrod. We will get deeper into this as we get to the beast who came out of the earth in the next chapter.

> WEB Rev 13:3b . . . the whole world was astonished and followed the beast. 4 They worshiped the dragon (the Devil), because he gave his authority to the beast, and they worshiped the beast, saying, "Who is like the beast? Who is able to make war with him?"

Nimrod was known as having great strength and as being undefeatable, being a giant and all things considered. However, on this occasion when the people marvel and it says, "Who is able to make war with him?" it is talking about how, not only he has returned from the dead, but he killed the unkillable—the two witnesses. For it previously said:

NAS REV 11:7 When they (the two witnesses) have finished their testimony, <u>the beast that comes up out of the abyss will make war with them, and overcome them and kill them.</u>

> WEB Rev 13:5 A mouth speaking great things and blasphemy was given to him. Authority to make war for forty-two months was given to him.

Again, the beast that came out of the sea has the same prophetic picture as the Devil himself. That is because in God granting the Devil his destiny and power, He has also granted that the Devil can give that power to his human agent, Nimrod, the beast and antichrist—the seed of Ham who survived the flood. There is no higher authority given to man on the earth than that of the four horseman and the four winds of destruction that God loosed as a part of His second judgment.

That is why the world marvels at our inability to challenge the beast and overcome. No one can defeat him! That is with the exception of Jesus, who through His miracles witnessed to us all, His power to save is greater than the Devil's power to destroy—He is greater in power than the four horsemen. When the purposes of God are served, it is Jesus alone who will make war and defeat him.

That authority to make war for 42 months (3-1/2 years) is an authority to (as it says in Daniel) shatter or crush the power of the holy people (the prostitute). In warring against the saints, Nimrod, the beast, will be destroying the seventh kingdom and setting himself up as the eighth. This time is the time of the great tribulation. It is made more clear in the next verse 13:6 (below)

> WEB Rev 13:6 *He opened his mouth for blasphemy against God, to blaspheme his name, and his dwelling, those who dwell in heaven. 7 It was given to him to make war with the saints, and to overcome them. Authority over every tribe, people, language, and nation was given to him. 8 All who dwell on the earth will worship him, everyone whose name has not been written from the foundation of the world in the book of life of the Lamb who has been killed. 9 If anyone has an ear, let him hear.*

"It was given to him to make war with the saints, and overcome them." Daniel heard the same thing when he was told:

> NAS DA 12:7 *I heard the man dressed in linen , who was above the waters of the river, as he raised his right hand and his left toward heaven, and swore by Him who lives forever that it would be for a time, times, and half a time; and as soon as they finish shattering the power of the holy people, all these events will be completed.*

And again in Revelation:

> Amp Rev 17:16 *And the ten horns that you saw, they and the beast will [be the very ones to] hate the harlot (the idolatrous woman); they will make her (the Church Corrupt) cheerless (bereaved, desolate), and they will strip her and eat up her flesh and utterly consume her with fire.*

Amp Rev 17:17 *For God has put it into their hearts to carry out His own purpose by acting in harmony in surrendering their royal power and authority to the beast, until the prophetic words (intentions and promises) of God shall be fulfilled.*

The *Church Corrupt* has been called four different names. It is typical in prophecy to refer to an individual by different names. In Daniel, the *Church Corrupt* is called, "the holy people," in Revelation, the *Church Corrupt* is called, "the great prostitute who rides the beast." Then later in Revelation, the *Church Corrupt* is referred to as, "the saints." Finally, in the end, Revelation calls the *Church Corrupt* none other than, "Babylon."

The little horn/the false prophet/beast out of the earth has a bigger share in destroying the Church during the great tribulation than one might imagine.

Sound absurd? The Catholic Church, by many accounts, are already responsible for the deaths of an estimated 60 million people. Fellow Christians are the lion's share of those they killed.

NIV Rev 13:10 *If anyone is to go into captivity,*

into captivity he will go.

If anyone is to be killed with the sword,

with the sword he will be killed.

This calls for patient endurance and faithfulness on the part of the saints

God makes clear to us the authority and power of the beast, as given by the Devil, futile to contend with. Nothing can save us from it if we are on planet earth, during those 3-1/2 years given to the beast. We would do much better to, if possible, hide than to challenge it by fighting during the great tribulation. These times are determined by God to purify the *Church Corrupt*. We can know it is true because it states that patient endurance and faithfulness on the part of the saints are required during this time that we are helpless but to endure while keeping our integrity intact.

So ends this prophetic picture worth a thousand words of the beast who comes out of the sea. It is after the 3-1/2 years of the great tribulation, or his 42 months to have unrestrained global power, that his time is through. He and his kingdom are punished most severely, climaxing with a battle against the Lord at Armageddon. After his defeat he is thrown alive into the lake of fire and he is no more a factor on any of God's creation ever again!

CHAPTER 4

The Beast Out of the Earth

WEB Rev 13:11 *I saw another beast coming up out of the earth. He had two horns like a lamb, and he spoke like a dragon.*

This second beast who comes up out of the earth is an individual. We see in the verses to come that this beast is also called the "false prophet." This prophetic picture of him, though short, has a lot of information concerning him. He is the spiritual minister of Nimrod's kingdom and is the one who works magic and genetics creating a body in order to bring Nimrod back from the dead to rule the earth. Being called a beast reflects that he is soulless as a beast, just as the first beast, Nimrod. Soulless in that they are spirit led (by the Devil himself) and not creatures of reason, nor sensitive to the feelings and needs of others. They are predatorial in nature, and lustful in gratifying their hunger for power—they are driven by instinctual desires.

The fact that he comes from the earth is a sign that he too is someone who comes back from the dead. Out of the earth is synonymous with out of the grave. There are a couple of Biblical verses which support this. In the verses above he has two horns which represent two times of power. Two horns has another meaning as well, which will be covered next as we develop interpretation of his prophetic profile or picture worth a thousand words. The next factor which supports this second beast is someone who returns from the dead is in verse 20:

NIV Rev 19:19 *Then I saw the beast and the kings of the earth and their armies gathered together to make war against the rider on the horse and his army.*

NIV Rev 19:20 <u>But the beast was captured, and with him the false prophet who had performed the</u> <u>miraculous signs on his behalf. With</u> *these signs he had deluded those who had received the* <u>mark of the beast and worshiped his image. The two of them were thrown alive into the fiery</u> <u>lake of burning sulfur.</u>

NIV Rev 19:21 The rest of them were killed with the sword that came out of the mouth of the rider on the horse (Jesus), and all the birds gorged themselves on their flesh.

To be thrown alive into the lake of fire is to suffer the "second death." This is what Jude was talking about when he said in Jude 1:12b (below):

NIV Jude 1:10 Yet these men speak abusively against whatever they do not understand; and what things they do <u>understand by instinct, like unreasoning animals</u>—these are the very things that destroy them.

NIV Jude 1:11 Woe to them! They have taken the way of Cain; they have rushed for profit into Balaam's error; they have been destroyed in Korah's rebellion.

NIV Jude 1:12 These men are blemishes at your love feasts, eating with you without the slightest qualm—shepherds who feed only themselves. They are clouds without rain, blown along by the wind (soulless, or spirit led); autumn trees, without fruit and <u>uprooted—twice dead.</u>

NIV Jude 1:13 They are wild waves of the sea, foaming up their shame; wandering stars, for whom blackest darkness has been reserved forever.

By saying, "autumn trees, without fruit" Jude is saying about these men that they are leaders who bear no fruit for God when it is the season for fruit to be ripe. "Uprooted—twice dead," this is such an interesting indictment Jude makes against these people. Only a person who follows Christ and knows the truth about life and death can understand what he is saying. "Uprooted", in other words, they will die because of their sins, losing their kingdom place and instead their disembodied soul will be assigned to the Abyss (bottomless pit) in Hades.

"Twice dead," on the day of judgment when all will be raised from the dead to face God and account for their lives, they will then suffer the ultimate punishment by being thrown alive into the lake of fire, forever. This is the second death. However, until the last day, the day of judgment, no living being resides in the lake of fire.

NIV Rev 20:11 Then I saw a great white throne and him who was seated on it. Earth and sky fled from his presence, and there was no place for them.

NIV Rev 20:12 And I saw the dead, great and small, standing before the throne (resurrected, given a body in order to face judgment), *and books were opened. Another book was opened, which is the book of life. The dead were judged according to what they had done as recorded in the books.*

NIV Rev 20:13 The sea gave up the dead that were in it, and death and Hades gave up the dead that were in them, and each person was judged according to what he had done.

NIV Rev 20:14 Then death and Hades were thrown into the lake of fire. The lake of fire is the second death.

NIV Rev 20:15 If anyone's name was not found written in the book of life, he was thrown into the lake of fire.

Only the beast/antichrist/Nimrod and the false prophet, we are told, will be confined there before the last day of judgment comes (verse Rev 20:11-15 [above]). From the time they are thrown in alive after their capture at the battle of Armageddon, they will be alone for a thousand years after the Lord's Kingdom of heaven comes down to the earth. It is then that the last day will happen and those who are judged to be condemned will also be thrown alive into the lake of fire joining them.

Therefore, for the second beast to be thrown alive into the lake of fire before the last day, as we are told in Rev 19:20 (above), by virtue means, that he had lived once before and was resurrected from being dead or disembodied.

We know that Nimrod who was, is not now, but will be, he comes out from among the dead on his way to his destruction, to the lake of fire (Rev 17:11). By knowing he died the first death, we know that Nimrod can only die by being thrown alive into the lake of fire for eternity because he already suffered the first death.

Accordingly, the false prophet who came out of the earth, the grave, and Nimrod, the antichrist, are the only ones who do not die at the battle of Armageddon. Instead of suffering a first death like all who follow them into this battle against the Lord, they are made to suffer the second death. For both to suffer the second death means that both had suffered the first death. The rest of humanity will wait 1,000 more years for the day of judgment when they too will be resurrected with a new body and be made to face the second death. Until then, the antichrist and the false prophet have the distinction of being alone in the lake of fire, 1,000 years before anyone else.

It says of him that he had two horns like a lamb. Many interpret this to mean that he will start out gentle like a lamb or a savior then suddenly turn vicious. This verse does not mean that at all. It is talking about him having two horns similar to a lamb, and not him being like a lamb.

To truly understand what it means when said, "two horns like a lamb," you must first of all understand some facts about sheep. When it comes to sheep there are ewe's, rams, lambs, and yearlings. A ewe is a female sheep. A ram is a male sheep. A yearling is a male or female sheep whose age is between one year old and two years old. Once it hits the two year mark it is no longer called a yearling and is considered a mature male or female sheep—ewe or ram. When it is below the one year mark in age, male or female, the sheep is considered a lamb. It is a baby sheep. As soon as it hits the one year mark it is no longer a baby, or lamb, but a yearling.

Above we are told the beast out of the earth will have horns like a lamb. When it says that, it is telling us not about his personality. Horns represent power. First of all, the horns of a lamb only last one year, because then the sheep is no longer a lamb. Secondly, their horns are like two little nubs or bumps poking out of their head. In other words, they are small. Alexander the Great and his empire was represented as a goat with a single "prominent" horn between its eyes. Alexander had acquired massive amount of territory as his empire. When that horn was broken off the goat, which signified the death of Alexander, four more grew in its place. Those four horns were the four generals who divided up Alexander's empire while it remained the Greek Empire.

In the case of the second beast or false prophet and unlike Alexander he has two horns like a lamb which are small. This speaks volumes! In the case of Alexander, the goat represented the Greek Empire, and the single horn of the goat was the power and God ordained destiny behind it, who was Alexander. That is until he died as prophetically represented by the horn having broken off. The empire remained and his four generals or horns rose up and became the power behind the empire which then continued unbroken.

This is not the case for the second beast out of the earth. The false prophet is the beast, and his two horns are his ordained destinies of granted power. The fact that this individual has two horns means he has two times of power, and two positions of power. Remembering back in Daniel, the false prophet/the second beast was given a prophetic profile which portrayed him (Pope Leo III of the Roman Catholic Church) as being a "little horn with eyes like a man, and a mouth which spoke boastful words" of which before it, three of the ten horns were uprooted. That "little horn" is one of the two little horns of the false prophet (the pope) making him the seventh kingdom of the beast.

Here in verse 11b it is said about the second beast that he had two little horns. First, why little? In the case of the pope prophetically pictured in Daniel represented as a little horn, the Papal States he was king over, by empire standards were relatively small. This is not withstanding the fact that he, the little horn, became prominent among the ten horns. Meaning, the little horn (the pope) became an authority over all the other horns. He became a ruler of the kings of the earth. That authority of the pope became the revived but now "Holy" Roman Empire.

What this told us is that because of that void of authority he stepped into, Pope Leo III of the Roman Catholic Church in Rome became the seventh shepherd/king of the Babylonian Empire. Likewise, according to the prophetic profile of the beast, Leo is the seventh head.

Micah told us there would be an eighth king who was one of the seven.

NIV Mic 5:5 And he (the Christ) will be their peace when the Assyrian (Nimrod) invades our land and marches through our fortresses. <u>We will raise against him seven shepherds, even eight leaders of men.</u>
NIV Mic 5:6 They will rule the land of Assyria with the sword, the land of Nimrod with drawn sword. He (the Christ) will deliver us from the Assyrian (Nimrod) when he invades our land and marches into our borders.

And again in Revelation:

NAS REV 17:9 " *Here is the mind which has wisdom. The seven heads* (of the beast) *are seven mountains on which the woman sits,*
NAS REV 17:10 *and they* (also) *are seven kings; five have fallen, one is, the other has not yet come; and when he comes, he must remain a little while.*

As of when John received this prophecy, five of the kings had come and gone, meaning they fulfilled their destiny and died. The sixth king was in power when he received this vision, for it says, "one is". That would be the king of the Roman Empire. Although the sixth king actually is Caesar Augusta who created the Roman Empire, he was dead when John received this prophecy. Notwithstanding, whoever succeeds him and sits on the seat of power that Augusta created and set in motion, remains the sixth king until the empire Augusta created is no more. So the reigning king (Caesar) of Augusta's empire when John received this prophecy is still the sixth king who "is."

It goes on to say that the other, which is the seventh king, "has not yet come." That is as of the time John received this prophecy. That seventh king is Pope Leo III and all the succeeding popes. As long as the seat of the popery continues, it is that seventh king which is the beast who came out of the earth. It says of him that he must remain a little while. A little while is not really saying that the length of time the seventh king reigns is only for a short time. It is more accurately saying that the seventh king will remain for an (extended) time. To date it has been 1,218 years (800 AD-2018 AD) since the seventh king, the pope, has ruled the empire of Babylon.

NAS REV 17:11 "*The beast which was and is not, is himself also an eighth and is one of the seven, and he goes to destruction.*

The beast himself, Nimrod, the founder of Babylon whose ordained destiny it was from God and from the Devil, will come back a second time and finally rule the entire globe as the eighth king. That is why there are not eight horns. The eighth king is the first horn of power granted to the beast himself, Nimrod.

What is important here is to take note that the small horn on one of the heads of the seven headed beast, is now identified as the second beast who came out of the earth.

He becomes the seventh king who revived the Roman Empire, and is also the false prophet. The eighth king is not a horn on one of the seven heads, nor is he one of the heads of the beast, but is the beast himself. He is Nimrod, along with all his appendages (horns, and heads, and crowns) which make up his legacy of power in the earth.

NAS REV 17:12 "The ten horns which you saw are ten kings who have not yet received a kingdom, but they receive authority as kings <u>with the beast for one hour.</u>
NAS REV 17:13 "These have one purpose, and they give their power and authority to the beast.
NAS REV 17:14 "These will wage war against the Lamb, and the Lamb will overcome them, because He is Lord of lords and King of kings, and those who are with Him are the called and chosen and faithful."

Again, that eighth king is Nimrod, who is the first king and founder of the Babylonian Empire back from the dead. When he comes, he will destroy the seventh kingdom of the beast in order to establish his dominance over Babylon and come into his destiny of being king of the entire world. Then he will set up ten leaders who will rule ten different districts of the world. The destruction of the seventh kingdom of which the pope is the seventh shepherd of, will be the great tribulation and persecution of the saints. However, the pope will bring Nimrod back to life and promote him as savior of the world and give his authority over to him—the beast. In the end, the pope will be the persecutor of the Christians in an effort to force them to worship the beast and the eighth king of Babylon.

NIV Da 7:23 "He gave me this explanation: 'The fourth beast is a fourth kingdom (or the sixth head of the beast out of the sea—the Roman Empire) *that will appear on earth. It will be different from all the other kingdoms <u>and will devour the whole earth, trampling it down and crushing it.</u>*

"The whole earth" is referring to the time (in the future) when Babylon and the beast out of the sea finally come into the fullness of their destinies. This fourth beast of Daniel is the Roman Empire. It is the sixth kingdom of Babylon and will evolve by changing forms rather than coming to an end and being replaced. It stays in the city of Rome and becomes the seventh kingdom which is the Roman Catholic Church who picks the pieces of the Roman Empire back up and revives it. Pope Leo III accomplishes this by forming an alliance or a confederacy of the ten nations (the ten horns he was prominent over) that were responsible for the defeat of the Roman Empire. Then, he turns that confederacy into the Holy Roman Empire. He chose and crowned one of those ten kings emperor (Charlemagne of the Franks), while positioning himself as the authority over the emperor and the other nine kings.

When the eighth kingdom comes after the seventh ushers in the returned Nimrod, the pope will turn his kingdom over to the beast. It is then that the first beast, Nimrod, will finally rule "the whole earth." Thus, the sixth, seventh, and eighth transition into each other and are virtually different faces of the (same) Roman Empire.

Note: The natural question that arises from this is that Revelation is calling the Roman Empire the sixth kingdom, whereas in Daniel there are only four and it is called the fourth kingdom (the fourth beast). Are these two prophetic visions talking about the same thing? The answer is yes! Revelation shows the entire prophetic profile of the beast and his legacy. Whereas in both Nebuchadnezzar's dream of the statue and Daniel's vision of the four beasts, they both were being shown what was relevant from their time forward. The three previous kingdoms of Babylon, or heads of the beast, had already passed. The Lord was sharing with Nebuchadnezzar and Daniel what the future held which was relevant to them from that time forward.

Verse 23 (above) was a summary statement about the fourth beast of Daniel. In the next verse 24 (below) it gives details of that fourth beast and how it eventually evolves in its forms before finally ruling the entire globe.

NIV Da 7:24 The ten horns are ten kings who will come from this kingdom. After them another king (horn) will arise, different from the earlier ones; he will subdue three kings (horns).
*NIV Da 7:25 He will speak against the Most High and oppress his saints and **try to change the set times and the laws.** The saints will be handed over to him for a time, times and half a time.*

This is comparable to the single horn of the ram which was Alexander the Great. That single horn being broken off was the death of Alexander. Then four horns grew up in its place replacing the one. Those four horns were the four generals of Alexander's who continued his empire but divided it into four sovereigns.

This sixth head of the beast, the Roman Empire, which suffers a fatal head wound (Rome being sacked and the empire destroyed), is taken over by ten other kings and kingdoms (ten horns). They did so just as the four did with Alexander's empire. However, the head, Rome, as the great city who rules the kings of the world is healed by the small horn that arises becoming the authority of the Holy Roman Empire and over the ten horns.

After the Roman Empire is broken, its territories become ruled by ten different kings (horns of power) who shared in the destruction of it. This is a matter of history for us. After this had happened, another (small) horn of power arises that was the pope who brought back or united once again these ten different kings and kingdoms under himself as the Holy Roman Empire. This act preserved Rome as being the great city who rules the kings of the world since the Roman Catholic Church (the great prostitute who rides the beast) sits on the city of seven hills (Rome). However, it was not before three of those ten kingdoms who opposed the pope and his climb to power were one by one eradicated and became no more. No other scenario in history matches this prophecy than how the Roman Catholic Church rose to its prominence to become a world power.

Here are examples of how the popery (the little horn) has tried to change the set times and laws: The popes have eliminated the second commandment. In addition, they have divided the tenth commandment in two in order to make up for having eliminated the second and still have ten. Next, the pope changed the commandment to honor the Sabbath Day, which is the last day of the week, Saturday, to the first day of the week, Sunday. This was first done by emperor Constantine as a civil observance, which in turn caused the Roman Church to follow suit (as it was meant to accomplish by Constantine). They also changed the observance of Passover, Good Friday, and Resurrection Day from the Hebrew calendar to the Gregorian calendar.

The Gregorian calendar system is named after Pope Gregory XIII, who like Constantine did not want to be dependent on the Jews and their calendar system.

Otherwise Christendom and the Roman Empire would continue to be subject to the Jews to know each year when Passover falls. In their calendar system of the Jews, the days of the year, and the holy days shift annually according to the lunar cycle. Whereas the Gregorian calendar goes according to the solar cycle and then the holy days are no longer (as much as) a moving target. This calendar system which is according to the sun and its cycle, is so much more palatable to the Romans because they worshiped the sun and held the day of the sun as sacred—Sunday. In fact, under Jupiter (Zeus/Satan) was Saturn who many regard as Nimrod, the sun god.

Changing to a calendar system that honored and worshiped the sun, Rome and Christendom would no longer have to be dependent on the Jews, waiting to hear from them when the holy days would fall each year on their calendar. Constantine saw it as demeaning, making Rome subject to the Jews as an authority to set the dates of the holy days. He would not have this, and the Roman Church followed suit. This is what Daniel is told that the little horn would do, and because the Catholic Church has done exactly that, it then gives another verification that the pope is the little horn.

Below is a Ten Commandments Comparison Chart to show how the popery has changed what God gave to Moses:

Ten Commandments Comparison Chart

Bible Ten Commandments		Catholic Ten Commandments	
1st	I *am* the LORD thy God, which have brought thee out of the land of Egypt, out of the house of bondage. Thou shalt have no other gods before me.	1st	I am the LORD thy God. Thou shalt have no strange gods before Me.
2nd	Exodus 20:4-6 You shall not make for yourself an idol in the form of anything in heaven above or on the earth beneath or in the waters below. You shall not bow down to them or worship them; for I, the LORD your God, am a jealous God, punishing the		Deleted. *(There is idolatry in the Papal system so the second Commandment has been deleted or sometimes it has been absorbed into the first.*

	children for the sin of the fathers to the third and fourth generation of those who hate me, but showing love to a thousand generations of those who love me and keep my Commandments.		*All remaining Commandments are therefore shifted along one count.)*
3rd	Thou shalt not take the name of the LORD thy God In vain; for the LORD will not hold him guiltless that taketh his name in vain.	**2nd**	Thou shalt not take the name of the LORD thy God in vain.
4th	Remember the sabbath day, to keep it holy. Six days shalt thou labour, and do all thy work: But the seventh day *is* the sabbath of the LORD your God: *in it* you shall not do any work, you, nor your son, nor your daughter, your manservant, nor your maidservant, nor your cattle, nor your stranger that *is* within your gates: For *in six* days the LORD made heaven and earth, the sea, and all that in them *is*, and rested the seventh day: wherefore the LORD blessed the sabbath day, and hallowed it.	**3rd**	Remember to keep holy the Sabbath day. *(The Sabbath is the fourth Commandment by normal count. The day to be kept is no longer mentioned since they changed the Sabbath to Sunday.)* *(Note: that God had more to say about the fourth Commandment than all others and with good reason. It is very important.)*
5th	Honour thy father and thy mother: that thy days may be long upon the land which the LORD thy God giveth thee.	**4th**	Honour thy father and thy mother.
6th	Thou shalt not kill.	**5th**	Thou shalt not kill.
7th	Thou shalt not commit adultery.	**6th**	Thou shalt not commit adultery.
8th	Thou shalt not steal.	**7th**	Thou shalt not steal.
9th	Thou shalt not bear false witness against thy neighbour.	**8th**	Thou shalt not bear false witness against thy neighbour.

10th	Thou shalt not covet thy neighbour's house, thou shalt not covet thy neighbour's wife, nor his manservant, nor his maidservant, nor his ox, nor his ass, nor any thing that *is* thy neighbour's.	9th	Thou shalt not covet thy neighbour's wife. (*The Tenth Commandment is split into two to get back to Ten Commandments.*)
		10th	Thou shalt not covet thy neighbour's goods.

2

The next thing concerning the horns like a lamb is the fact that they only last for a season, or a one year cycle. After that they can no longer be referred to as lamb horns. The time of the antichrist and the false prophet Jesus refers to, in the book of Revelation, as their "hour of power." Which again, is a cycle of time like the one year cycle of a lamb. The horns of power of the beast out of the earth do not have time to mature into something larger as those of a yearling sheep because it would need more time.

Concerning the two horns (of power) of the beast out of the earth: As outlined before, each horn represents two different times and/or two different powers/roles granted him. In Daniel, there rose up a little horn on the head of a beast which was the Roman Empire and who already had ten horns. That eleventh and little horn had eyes like a human and a mouth which speaks boastful words. He revived the Roman Empire. That little horn in Daniel is one of the two horns like a lamb of the beast out of the earth in Revelation, however, he has a second horn of power too.

1) One horn of power was to revive the head (or legacy) of the beast which had a fatal wound—the Roman Empire. Rome was the head of the Roman Empire. Having been overrun and conquered by its enemies was its fatal wound. Pope Leo III breathed it back to life when he organized its conquerors, uniting them into the Holy Roman Empire. In doing so, the popery became the authority over the kings of the earth, making him the seventh king of Babylon.

2) The second horn of power of the beast who came out of the earth will be to revive

from the dead and empower the person who is the beast and antichrist, Nimrod. The little horn with eyes and a mouth/the pope/false prophet/beast out of the earth will give the breath of life to the image (the body) he creates in the temple, for Nimrod to come back from the dead.

The first horn of power was God granting the pope the power to revive the Roman Empire from its fatal head wound—the sacking of Rome. This kept Rome the great city that rules the kings of the earth. The second horn of power was God granting the pope (the beast out of the earth) the power to revive the first beast (out of the sea) from a fatal wound—death. Both of these horns of power position the pope of the Roman Catholic Church to be the most powerful individual in the kingdom of the beast.

In Daniel we get more details about one of the horns like a lamb of the beast who came out of the earth. That one horn of his represents his rise to become the seventh shepherd/king of the seventh head and kingdom of the beast out of the sea. His sinful and power hungry heart combined with that horn of power made it his God granted destiny to become the authority over the revived Holy Roman Empire (the other ten horns).

The second of the two horns of the beast out of the earth is the role of the false prophet of the returned beast. The seventh kingdom consisting of the *Church Corrupt* is destroyed upon Nimrod's return from the dead of which the pope is the king of. However, the pope's second role or horn of power is that of the false prophet, which means he escapes the destruction of his kingdom, the Church, during the great tribulation. Why? Because he instead becomes the very one who raises the first beast, Nimrod, from the dead and causes, even forcing under penalty of death, the whole world to worship the beast. That especially includes the Christians left behind with him, who he is the Holy See over. Doing so while performing miracles on the behalf of the antichrist to demonstrate his great spiritual authority.

NIV Rev 17:6 I saw that the woman was drunk with the blood of the saints, the blood of those who bore testimony to Jesus.

Hard to believe? Since 800 AD when Pope Leo III, the false prophet, became the seventh king of Babylon and the Catholic Church had become the seventh kingdom, they have been responsible for taking an estimated 60 million lives in the name of Jesus. That is the very same Jesus who had the power to stop Himself from being killed by His enemies but did not, and refused to allow His followers to defend Him. He even healed the wound of the one who Peter struck to prevent Jesus' arrest. Jesus stated this:

Amp Jn 18:36 . . . My kingdom (kingship, royal power) belongs not to this world. If My kingdom were of this world, My followers would have been fighting to keep Me from being handed over to the Jews. But as it is, My kingdom is not from here (this world); [it has no such origin or source].

The overwhelming majority of the deaths the pope and Catholic Church are responsible for were Christians and Jews. In fact, they have genocide whole cultures and villages of Christians. We see below what Jesus said in Revelation that the pope will do as the false prophet of the beast/antichrist:

WEB Rev 13:12 He (the false prophet) *exercises all the authority of the first beast on his behalf. He makes the earth and those who dwell in it to worship the first beast, whose fatal wound was healed.*

Verse 12 (above) is a summary statement, then verse 13 and on give context and details to verse 12.

WEB Rev 13:13 He performs great signs, even making fire come down out of the sky to the earth in the sight of people. 14 He deceives the people who dwell on the earth because of the signs he was granted to do on behalf of the first beast; saying to those who dwell on the earth, that they should make an image to the beast who had the sword wound and lived.

It is the pope as the false prophet of the beast, who will prepare for the day he enters the temple and performs abominations which bring Nimrod back from the dead, by first making treaties with many nations. In the backdrop the two witnesses are preaching in power. They back up their words with signs and wonders which make the people suffer, however, they also make it impossible to be ignored. They will stifle the goings on of the people on the earth as Moses did in Egypt. The pope as the false prophet will use his international influence and the occasion of the two witnesses to have the needed support of the world to bring Nimrod back from the dead.

The false prophet will, like the magicians in pharaoh's court, duplicate the miracles of the two witnesses. However, just like the magicians in pharaoh's court, his miracles will be impotent, unlike those of the two witnesses. The two witnesses will prove themselves unkillable and the people of the world will become one heart and voice together in their desperation to bring an end to them. The time is ripe, the people will beg the pope for a solution concerning the two witnesses and how to kill the unkillable.

His solution, he will tell the world, is to bring Nimrod, a giant and the vanquisher of Yahweh, back from the grave and he will bring an end to those two witnesses. He will kill the unkillable. He will save the people of the world from them. In their defiance of God, their desperation of being set free of them, and like the unanimous decision of the people in the cities of Sodom and Gomorrah and all their surrounding villages, the whole world will do anything at any cost, no matter how evil, to get rid of the two witnesses. The pope and false prophet will take full advantage and commit atrocities, abominations which have not been preformed since before the flood, which will result in bringing Nimrod back to life in God's own temple.

> WEB Rev 13:15 It was given to him to give breath to it, to the image of the beast, that the image of the beast should both speak, and cause as many as wouldn't worship the image of the beast to be killed.

Then the pope as the false prophet while supported by all the people of the earth, will enter the temple and make a body for Nimrod, the giant, to come back among the living. The false prophet's promise to the world is that, what he brings to life will kill the unkillable—the two witnesses. Indeed, after the pope gives the breath to the image of the beast he created, the beast/antichrist will leave the temple to war with the two witnesses, and kill them.

The whole world will celebrate, even exchanging gifts, we are told, because of the relief they enjoy upon the death of the two witnesses. Nimrod will have finally demonstrated his original boast that he would protect the world from Yahweh. After the two witnesses raise back to life, three and a half days later, they depart this earth. Just as the angels saved righteous Lot and his family from the destruction of Sodom and Gomorrah, the Holy Spirit will bring with Him the *Church Pure* when He likewise departs this world leaving it in a state of a global desolation and under the absolute control of the beast.

Daniel describes the same event about the false prophet in greater detail:

NIV Da 9:26 *After the sixty-two 'sevens,' the Anointed One* (Jesus) *will be cut off* (killed) *and will have nothing. The people of the ruler who will come* (the false prophet and beast who come out of the earth)*will destroy the city and the sanctuary. The end will come like a flood: War will continue until the end, and desolations have been decreed.*

Verse 26 (above) is a mouthful; in that it covers thousands of years of history past and future. At the end of the 62-7's is when Jesus is killed. The 7-7's had already been fulfilled by the time the 62-7's began. In fact, there was a gap of time between the time the 7-7's were complete and the 62-7's began. The 7-7's began when the Jews were released from Babylonian captivity in order to rebuild the temple.

"The people of the ruler who will come . . ." is talking about the Romans (the people) who in 70AD destroyed Jerusalem, the temple, and for the longest time Jews were banned from entering Jerusalem. This is worded in a very significant way. When it reads, "who will come" it is not referring to the people, as in, the people who will come. It is referring to the ruler who will come. The people of the ruler who is to come will destroy Jerusalem long before he (the ruler) comes. That ruler who will come is the false prophet. His people are the Roman Empire. The Roman Empire, the sixth kingdom of the beast, is being tied to the seventh kingdom who, by this wording, the false prophet/pope is the king of.

The reason the sixth and seventh kingdoms are tied together like this is twofold: The seventh kingdom doesn't defeat the sixth, meaning the Roman Church does not defeat the Roman Empire. No! The seventh revives it, healing it (the head wound) and the pope/false prophet takes ownership of the empire.

Question: How do we know that the "ruler who will come" is talking about the false prophet/pope, and not just the emperor of the Roman Empire who was in power at 70 AD when Jerusalem was destroyed? Because in Daniel it continues to talk about this ruler who will come and says about him:

NIV Da 9:27a He (the ruler who will come) *will confirm a covenant with many for one 'seven.' In the middle of the 'seven' he will put an end to sacrifice and offering.*

This is talking about the last seven of the 70-7's which has yet to come. We are in a gap between the 62-7's and the final 1-7. That gap we currently are in, and has so far lasted about 2,000 years, is the Church Age. The false prophet/pope of the Roman Catholic Church will make diplomatic treaties and alliances with some nations along the lines of the United Nations, or NATO, in order to give those nations a voice among the super powers of the world. However, it will be an alliance which is spiritually based, giving acceptance without conformity to the laws of God by twisting around Bible truths.

In 70 AD after Jerusalem was destroyed by Rome, the Jewish historian, Josephus, described the ruins as resulting in a desert. It was leveled so thoroughly, he stated, that anyone passing by would not believe that there was once a city on that site. It was exactly as Jesus predicted when He said:

NIV Mt 24:2 "Do you see all these things?" he asked. "I tell you the truth, <u>not one stone here will be left on another;</u> every one will be thrown down."

Sometime after its destruction, the Roman Emperor Hadrian rebuilt Jerusalem. On the temple site he built a temple to Jupiter, who the Greeks refer to as, Zeus, and of whom Jesus told us is Satan. There they made sacrifices to him. Hadrian made it illegal for a Jew to enter the city under penalty of death. He made circumcision against the law. He also renamed Jerusalem, "Aelia Capitolina." It then became a city dedicated to Satan and Jupiter by Hadrian. If you can imagine the sacred ground of God and where His people worshiped Him was defiled in God's absence and used to do that which is appalling and insulting to the One God.

The Capitoline Hill is one of the seven hills of Rome. It is the hill where the Roman's built a temple to worship Jupiter (Satan). At the base of that hill is a temple to Saturn (the sun god) who is Nimrod. The word "capitol" comes from the name of the hill Capitoline which means head or summit.

Aelia Capitolina has since then returned to the name, Jerusalem, Israel and Jerusalem are now the home of the Jews. However, Jerusalem is still under a desolation, an absence of the presence of God. For on the temple site in Jerusalem there sits the second most sacred masque of the Muslims.

Note: It's interesting that the Devil and the great city of Babylon, Rome, attempted to make a temple for the Devil and the antichrist where the temple of God was. They are drawn to it because of fate. It's like they're trying to force something to happen before it is time. Rome was the great city of Babylon who rules the kings of the earth during the Roman Empire, the sixth kingdom of the beast.

Rome continued to be the great city of Babylon who rules the kings of the earth for the seventh kingdom, the Catholic Church. According to God's plan from the beginning it is to be on His holy mountain that He will crush the Assyrian/beast/antichrist. For that to take place, Jerusalem becomes the great city of Babylon who rules the kings of the earth when the pope raises Nimrod from the dead as well as the eighth and final kingdom.

Jerusalem was a sacred city for the Lord and His people, it was a place to worship Him. Nevertheless, after 70 AD Jerusalem became a sacred place for Satan and the antichrist to be worshiped. However, this was not the time designated by God for the global and end times expression of the line of offspring of the Devil. Because of their rejection and murder of the Lord, their Messiah, the presence of God left the stone temple and gave it over to Babylon. However, His Spirit presence continues to reside in the earth in temples of flesh, in all the believers who are in *spiritual union* with Him. It was neither the time when the Lord would destroy the Assyrian on His holy mountain, for he had not yet come back to life. Nevertheless, the Bible tells us that the temple of Yahweh will be rebuilt in the future to serve as the stage God has determined the end to transpire at.

NIV Da 9:27 He (the false prophet) *will confirm a covenant with many for one 'seven.' In the middle of the 'seven' he will put an end to sacrifice and offering. <u>And on a wing</u>* (pinnacle or height of his abominations at) <u>*of the temple he will set up an abomination that causes desolation, until the end that is decreed is poured out on him.*</u>

Although the overwhelming majority of the nations resist like the Romans, no power on earth has been able to stop the Jews from returning to Israel and Jerusalem. No one can stop the plans of God from unfolding the way He has decreed.

MSG Psalm 46:6 Godless nations rant and rave, kings and kingdoms threaten, but Earth does anything he *(God) says.*

Soon in the future, and as sure as all Biblical prophecy comes true, the temple of the true God will be rebuilt. The false prophet—the pope of the Catholic Church will bring the Assyrian (Saturn) back to life on the holy mountain in the temple of the Lord for that final showdown. It will be just as we are told in Daniel, above.

Revelation has as its main subject the *Church Corrupt* in the next or third narrative of Revelation which starts with chapter 17. The entire chapter is dedicated to her (the *Church Corrupt*) and her relationship with the beast. When it starts out, it gives us a prophetic profile of the *Church Corrupt* in the typical fashion of the second narrative. That profile is a prophetic picture worth a thousand words showing how she empowers herself with the beast (with Babylon).

NIV Rev 17:3b . . . *There I saw a woman sitting on a scarlet beast that was covered with blasphemous names and had seven heads and ten horns.*

Scarlet is the color of the authority of the Roman Catholic Church. She is sitting on the beast. If you can imagine, she rides the beast with bit in its mouth and the bridal in her hands making this beast her beast of burden. The *Church Corrupt* is shown as empowering herself with the power of the beast, the power of Babylon.

NIV Rev 17:9 . . . *The seven heads are <u>seven hills on which the woman sits.</u>*

NIV Rev 17:10 *They are also seven kings. Five have fallen, one is, the other has not yet come; but when he does come, he must remain for a little while.*

The beast has seven heads which, among other things, represent the seven hills of Rome. Rome and the Roman Empire is the sixth kingdom of Babylon. The city Rome is that empire's head or chief city from which the empire is ruled, where its seat of authority is (Caesar's throne). This makes Rome the "great city." The great city is another name for Babylon and the seat (or city) of its power. It is the city which rules the kings of the world. The great city has moved from Babylon in Persia to a city in Assyria, back to Babylon, to Greece, then to Rome.

The *Church Corrupt* is seen "sitting on the beast." We are next told (above) that she sits on the seven hills (of Rome/the great city of the Roman Empire). She, the woman and great prostitute who is the *Church Corrupt* was given lands, properties and buildings in Rome by the Roman Empire, some of which are currently called the Vatican City. She is empowered, protected, and enriched by the Roman Empire (which is the sixth head of the beast). For this, God is calling her, the *Church Corrupt*, "the great prostitute." Again, this is her state at the beginning of her prophetic picture worth a thousand words.

However, the very end of this chapter which is devoted to her prophetic characterization says something very curious in this final statement:

NIV Rev 17:18 *The woman you saw is the great city that rules over the kings of the earth."*

Rome was the great city of the Roman Empire from where they ruled the kings of the earth from (the head). The seven heads are the seven hills of Rome. This is where the Catholic Church is seated, in Rome. That is why it says she rides the beast, making the Roman Empire her beast of burden. And she is seated on the seven hills, the great city and head of the Roman Empire.

What this last statement of the prophetic picture of the *Church Corrupt* tells us is that; the Church started out prostituting herself by being empowered, protected, and enriched by Babylon (the Roman Empire and sixth kingdom of the beast). However, in the end, she became Babylon, the great city, the seventh kingdom of the beast. Chapter 17 ends by saying the woman, not the Roman Empire, is the kingdom and king of the great city, who rules the kings of the earth. The Roman Church became the seventh kingdom or head of the beast but is still seated in Rome, the city on seven hills. She is seated and rules from the city of seven hills, Rome.

This tells us of two transitions. The first being the *Church Corrupt* transitions from prostituting herself to the Roman Empire to becoming the Holy Roman Empire. The second transition is that although the great city remains Rome, Babylon transferring from the sixth kingdom of the beast, the Roman Empire, to the seventh kingdom of the beast, which is the *Church Corrupt* (the Holy Roman Empire and Roman Catholic Church).

NIV Rev 17:10 *They are also seven kings. Five have fallen, one is, the other has not yet come; but when he does come, he must remain for a little while.*

The sixth king who "is" at the time John received this prophecy, was the emperor of the Roman Empire. That seventh king who (at John's time) had not yet come but when he did would remain for a little while, is the pope of the Catholic Church starting in 800AD. The pope is the false prophet and seventh king. And will be the one who transfers Babylon to the eighth king, the risen Nimrod (the first king of Babylon).

The "other" or seventh king who has not yet come but when he does he must remain for a "little" while, is also referring to the short time of total power the beast, Nimrod, will have and share with the false prophet/pope; who brings him back to life. In spite of the fact that the king of the seventh kingdom, the pope of the Catholic Church, has been in power over Babylon since 800 AD, the total and absolute power of global domination which he shares with the beast is only for a little time. It is the "hour" of power (Rev 17:12) given to the beast, false prophet, and the ten kings ruling the entire globe. That hour is a seven year period. That time of power is for certain "little" in this reference. It is a half hour (Rev 8:1), a half of a seven year cycle that they will be able to do all that they please, once the false prophet raises Nimrod from the dead.

To be exact that little time is 3-1/2 years, and it is the second horn like a lamb that the beast out of the earth has been granted. It is just like a lamb in that his horns are small and he has only one cycle of time—an hour, a seven year period. The remaining 3-1/2 years heaven will be active again and punish the kingdom of the beast so severely that it can hardly function.

NIV Rev 17:11 *The beast who once was, and now is not, is an eighth king. He belongs to the seven* (or is one of the seven) *and is going to his destruction.*

Daniel tells us that it is this false prophet who makes treaties with many nations and who stops the sacrifices in the temple, that will raise up the beast from out of the Abyss, in the temple of God.

NIV Da 9:27 He (the false prophet) *will confirm a covenant with many for one 'seven.' In the middle of the 'seven' he will put an end to sacrifice and offering. And on a wing of the temple* (at the pinnacle or height of his activities in the temple) *he will set up an abomination that causes desolation, until the end that is decreed is poured out on him.*

That end that is decreed to be poured out on him, the false prophet, is being thrown alive into the lake of fire. He will be thrown in, alongside Nimrod, after the battle of Armageddon, 1,000 years before the lake of fire is open for business (as it were).

NIV Rev 17:7 *Then the angel said to me: "Why are you astonished? I will explain to you the mystery of the woman and of the beast she rides, which has the seven heads and ten horns.* NIV Rev 17:8 *The beast, which you saw, once was, now is not, and will come up out of the Abyss and go to his destruction. The inhabitants of the earth whose names have not been written in the book of life from the creation of the world will be astonished when they see the beast, because he once was, now is not, and yet will come.*

"The beast" will come up out of the Abyss and "go to his destruction" verifies that along with the false prophet, Nimrod will also be thrown alive into the lake of fire. That is their end! This all shows how the sixth and seventh kingdoms are tied together. One was a transition from the other as being Babylon. The legs of iron turned into the feet of iron mixed with clay. Finally, the seventh transitions into the time of the beast, the eighth king Babylon who was the first.

NIV Da 2:31 *"You looked, O king, and there before you stood a large statue—an enormous, dazzling statue, awesome in appearance.*

NIV Da 2:32 *The head of the statue was made of pure gold, its chest and arms of silver, its belly and thighs of bronze,*

NIV Da 2:33 <u>*its legs of iron, its feet partly of iron and partly of baked clay.*</u>

NIV Da 2:34 *While you were watching, a rock was cut out, but not by human hands. It struck the statue on its feet of iron and clay and smashed them.*

That rock striking the feet of clay mixed with iron is the Lord coming against Babylon in the *Church Corrupt*, using the risen beast to do it with. That occasion is the time of the great tribulation. Then He comes against Babylon in the world as described below.

NIV Da 2:35 *Then the iron, the clay, the bronze, the silver and the gold were broken to pieces at the same time and became like chaff on a threshing floor in the summer. The wind swept them away without leaving a trace. But the rock that struck the statue became a huge mountain and filled the whole earth.*

The result is the Lord utterly destroys Babylon and comes with a huge mountain with the New Jerusalem on it bringing His celestial humans—His bride—with Him to rule the whole world for a thousand years.

Here is a prophetic dream given to the author:

Dream: Saddam Hussein's Rise Back To Power
September 18, 2005

Saddam Hussein having lost control of his own country, became sympathetic for the cause of several different countries (in reality, at the time of this dream, he had been imprisoned and a little over a year later executed). He took up the cause of one very small country, Cuba. He used his notoriety and experience to campaign for them. He seemed to only have their benefit in mind. As well as securing their position in league with the several different countries. However, I saw that he had ulterior motives. At just the right moment he planned to take control of the small country. Then using the influence he helped that small country achieve, he helped others do the same. The next step of his plan helped them form an alliance like the United Nations or NATO so that together they had a greater and more influential (international) voice.

His next step was to take control of the league of nations he was helping and forming. Then through gaining power over the league he somehow took control of the other countries in the league and they became like vassals to him. Having done that he took back control of his own country once again. I could see that he would become more powerful than when he originally was with just his own country. All the while he looked like he was unselfishly helping campaign for other small and insignificant countries, however, he eventually became an international threat.

He had rage against the world who had caused him to lose his nation in the first place. The countries involved went along because they thought he was sincere in helping them with his notoriety and influence. They were blinded by the seeming benefits and ignored all the warnings. As well, the world ignored his whole rise because they never believed he could become successful or that his activities in the smallest countries would ever be a threat. In addition, they ignored all my prophetic warnings until it was too late.

This dream is about the rise of the false prophet. In dreams, God will sometimes use individuals you know for certain traits to represent the true subject of the dream. In interpreting dreams one has to be aware of that. Knowing this goes a long way in helping one understand what traits in the true subject of the dream God is highlighting and communicating. However, that leaves it to interpret who the true subject of the dream is. There are always clues in the dream to help you interpret if the subject in the dream is that actual person or a representation of that person. For example, it can be assumed that the Lord knows the fate of Saddam Hussein being jailed and then executed, however, the dream shows him as someone doing the things that the false prophet is destined to do. This assumption helps us understand this dream is not about Saddam Hussein, but that certain traits, activities, and motives he possesses give us insight into those of the real but unidentified subject, as well as his traits, activities, and motives.

Note: This is a great method the Lord uses because of the following: It is almost impossible to believe the pope of the Catholic Church to be a tyrant who wants to rule the entire world and bring back Nimrod from the dead. However, God shows us in a spiritual sense what his heart is really like. The picture of the pope's true heart is more like what we know Saddam Hussein to be. It is not what the position of the pope and his rhetoric would have us believe about him.

Note: One might say that since the beast out of the earth is someone who comes back to life, then maybe it is Saddam Hussein and he will come back to life to fulfill this dream about the rise of the false prophet. In answer, it is impossible for this to be the case. Saddam Hussein and the throne of his regime would have to reach back to the destruction of the Roman Empire and be responsible for reviving it after it was destroyed, according to Daniel and Revelation. Otherwise prophecy would be inaccurate. In reality, his regime reaches back in Saddam Hussein's lifetime only.

Historically that distinction can go to only one king and kingdom, the pope, his Catholic Church, and the Holy Roman Empire the popery is in authority over. Likewise, in order for the seven kingdoms of Babylon to be unbroken since the four horsemen were released a few generations after the flood, the succession of those seven kingdoms would still need to be represented and in power today. Again, that is the Roman Catholic Church who remains today in all its pomp and they are the only ones who qualify to be the fulfillment of that prophecy. That is even if the Roman Catholic Church is currently only a mere remnant left of the Holy Roman Empire with the kings and nations under the pope's authority. That remnant (the pope and the Roman Catholic Church) was the creator (reviver) and final authority of the Holy Roman Empire and still exists to this day, in authority as a sovereign.

God using a different person to represent the real subject in a dream might look like this: Let's say that you have a dream about your uncle, but in the dream he was represented as a teacher from your past who was mean and uncaring. By doing this God would be helping you see and feel in that place beyond words (in the instinctual part of your spirit) that your uncle is mean and uncaring even if he wants to teach you something. As a result, you would feel something about your uncle that you did not trust or would cause you to not be so open to him. It would be something that you would not be able to put your finger on, but an instinct or a gut feeling you would have when considering receiving help from him. In this way, God protects you from him even when in your mind you are naive and see no reason that you should not trust him, or are blinded by your love and loyalty for family.

Or perhaps you have a dream about your father who you love and respect. Who, in the dream, you trusted while going through difficult circumstances. According to the dream and because you did trust him, he was able to saved you from those circumstances you were stuck in. However, it was not your father in the dream. Your father was representing someone in your dream who God wants you to trust when some real life circumstances befall you and God knows that person will be a good help.

Then later, when you go through the trying circumstances God foreknew, and when that person your father represented in your dream comes around, something inside you, in that place beyond words, will feel like you can trust him as you did your father. This will occur even if you do not interpret the meaning of your dream, but it will give you a certain and intuitive feeling that will cause you to trust and rely on that person which are beyond or separate from the reason and logic of the mind. In fact, it will still take place even if you don't recall the dream or remember it the moment you wake up. Planting seeds in our spirit through dreams is one of the ways God uses for influencing, guiding, and protecting us in our lives—even speaking to us.

NIV Job 33:12 "*. . .for God is greater than man.*

NIV Job 33:13 *Why do you complain to him that he answers none of man's words*

NLT Job 33:13 *. . . You say, 'He does not respond to people's complaints.'*

NLT Job 33:14 *But God speaks again and again, though people do not recognize it.*

NLT Job 33:15 *He speaks in dreams, in visions of the night when deep sleep falls on people as they lie in bed.*

NLT Job 33:16 *He whispers in their ear and terrifies them with his warning.*

NLT Job 33:17 *He causes them to change their minds; he keeps them from pride.*

NLT Job 33:18 *He keeps them from the grave, from crossing over the river of death.*

Saddam Hussein was a dictator of Iraq, he was defeated, and executed for his crimes against humanity in December of 2006. The dream is not talking about him. It is talking about the false prophet. Why use him in the dream? A couple of reasons: He was a dictator and tyrant although it appeared that he was saving the people of his nation in his ambition to gain power. Most importantly, his country was small and weak but he wanted to make it a world power and finally an empire, by taking other nations.

Next, Saddam Hussein was determined to bring Babylon back to its former glory. In fact, he had rebuilt the city Babylon on its old foundations. He rebuilt its walls, and gates just as it had been in antiquity. He collected artifacts and art from that era in order to replicate the city authentically, and create a museum with exhibits from that era of former glory. The bricks that were used to rebuild had stamped on them "Saddam Hussein son of Nebuchadnezzar." However, Babylon, the "great city that rules the kings of the earth" has moved to Rome and is not on the site of the original city named Babylon.

About two years after the new pope Francis took office in 2014/15 he did exactly what the dream portrayed the false prophet would do. He took Cuba, an atheist government nation and reconciled it to some degree with the United States through President Obama. This prophetic dream verified the office of pope will produce the false prophet. Likewise, the Lord is calling the pope Saddam Hussein. Or a type of Saddam Hussein, with an evil heart as his. This would be hard to believe of a pope, however, this is how the Lord characterizes the heart and motives of the popery who desire to bring Nimrod back to life and dominate the entire globe in rebellion to the Lord.

NIV Da 9:27b *And on a wing* (or pinnacle) *of the temple he will set up an abomination that causes desolation, until the end that is decreed is poured out on him* (the pope and false prophet)."'

NIV Da 12:10 *Many will be purified, made spotless and refined, but the wicked will continue to be wicked. None of the wicked will understand, but those who are wise will understand.*

The above verse is talking about the results of the great tribulation. It is saying that the wise will understand why they must endure the great tribulation. Mainly that if they endure it without taking the mark of the beast or worshiping him, or giving up their testimony of Christ, they will be saved. However, it also says those who at heart are evil, the tribulation will bring the worst out of them and show their hearts for what they are. They will do anything it takes to survive or to take advantage of the times for personal gain. Again in Daniel, it says this in support of verse 12:10:

Amp Da 11:34 *Now when they fall, they shall receive a little help. Many shall join themselves to them with flatteries and hypocrisies.*

Amp Da 11:35 *And some of those who are wise, prudent, and understanding shall be weakened and fall, [thus, then, the insincere among the people will lose courage and become deserters. It will be a test] to refine, to purify, and to make those among [God's people] white, even to the time of the end, because it is yet for the time [God] appointed.*

What it says in verse 35 above, actually is the point of the great tribulation. To offer up one last test to show a true heart towards God as opposed to an insincere, and selfish self-centered heart that loves God by profession only.

NIV Da 12:11 *"From the time that the daily sacrifice is abolished and the abomination that causes desolation is set up, there will be 1,290 days.*

This verse tells us that it is not until the 1-7 of the 70-7's is complete that the end and great tribulation come. That is not withstanding that the false prophet will use his international influence to put an end to the animal sacrifices in the temple at the midpoint of the last 7. What that means is that from the midpoint 3-1/2 years into the last seven years there will be no activity in the temple until after that last seven is complete. It will be 1,260 days from the time the sacrifices are forced to stop that the 1-7 will come to an end. It will be 1,290 days from the time the sacrifices are forced to stop before the false prophet enters into the temple to do his evil magic and bring Nimrod, the beast and antichrist, back to life. It is laid out by the day to Daniel.

NIV Da 12:12 *Blessed is the one who waits for and reaches the end of the 1,335 days.*

The 1,335th day after the midpoint of the last seven or from the time the sacrifices are forced to stop, is when the two witnesses had already been killed and then raised from the dead 3-1/2 days later. On the 1,335th day they are called up to heaven, along with them goes the presence of God (His Spirit) taken away from the earth, as well as the rapture of the *Church Pure.*

The presence of the Lord is no longer in a temple of stone fixed on a foundation in Jerusalem, but in temples of flesh around the entire world in those who host His Spirit through their union with Him. Consequently, if the Holy Spirit departs this world, leaving it in a global desolation, He will have to choose either to abandon the many people who host His Spirit, or to take those in true union with Him to Heaven before His Father. This is what Jesus promised concerning this very situation:

Amp Jn 14:15 If you [really] love Me, you will keep (obey) My commands.

Amp Jn 14:16 And I will ask the Father, and He will give you another Comforter (Counselor, Helper, Intercessor, Advocate, Strengthener, and Standby), that He may remain with you forever—

Amp Jn 14:17 The Spirit of Truth, Whom the world cannot receive (welcome, take to its heart), because it does not see Him or know and recognize Him. But you know and recognize Him, for He lives with you [constantly] and will be in you.

Amp Jn 14:18 I will not leave you as orphans [comfortless, desolate, bereaved, forlorn, helpless]; I will come [back] to you.

Above, Jesus is talking about the fact that in His physical body He will depart the world as a result of His crucifixion. However, He assures those who obey Him that he will not leave them in the world on their own, He will not leave those who obey Him and host His Spirit within them in a state of desolation—an absence of the Holy Spirit. He makes a direct promise that He will come back to them by His Spirit and take up residence within them. He is adamant in saying He will not leave us as orphans, but return not in the body but by His Spirit in order to reside within us.

Amp Jn 14:19 Just a little while now, and the world will not see Me any more, but you will see Me; because I live, you will live also.

Now in verse 19 and 20 Jesus makes a leap in time beyond when He is killed and returns to the world in Spirit, occupying the temples of flesh of those who love and obey Him. He now makes reference to the day the great tribulation begins with a global desolation, when the two witnesses are called up. "The world will not see Me anymore . . . "

Jesus Himself taught us that God is Spirit (Jn 4:24). People in the world may think of Him as not here because He died to His earthly body. However, that is not how the Father and the Lord think of themselves. Jesus has not left this world when He lost His earthly body, but by His Spirit and while residing in the temples of flesh called His Church (pure), He remains in the earth as literally as He was before He was killed. This is not withstanding that in His celestial (resurrected) body He also sits at the right hand of the Father. Nevertheless, the Father and the Son see the Lord as not having departed this world. To them the Spirit is more real than the body. At one time, the Lord had one body in the world—Jesus. Now, however, the fullness of His person and His power is in the earth in the countless bodies which comprise His bride. As it says:

Amp Eph 1:22 *And He* (the Father) *has put all things under His feet and has appointed Him the universal and supreme Head of the* church [a headship exercised throughout the church],
Amp Eph 1:23 *Which is His body, the fullness of Him Who fills all in all [for in that body lives the full measure of Him Who makes everything complete, and Who fills everything everywhere with Himself].*

When the time of the beast and antichrist comes, the world will not see Him anymore—not by His Spirit, and not in the temples of flesh His Spirit is embodied with.

Amp Jn 14:20 *At that time [when that day comes] you will know [for yourselves] that I am in My Father, and you [are] in Me, and I [am] in you.*

"At that time when that day comes" What time/day is that? That day and time is when the Church Age is complete and the two witnesses have completed their work. Then, because of the abominations performed by the false prophet to bring back a giant, and because the whole world follows the risen Nimrod, the Lord will depart this world leaving it in a global desolation—an absence of the presence of God by His Spirit.

It is on that day when that time comes that He leaves the world, and because Jesus promised the Holy Spirit will be with us forever and He would not leave us like orphans, is when we will know for ourselves . . . How will that be the case? It will be the case because those in obedient union with the Spirit of Christ will suddenly find themselves clothed with a celestial body standing before the Father and the Son in heaven. When the rapture happens, those in union will realize God's Spirit is in Jesus, and their Spirit is in them, because when it departs the world and returns to heaven, they come with and in an instant find themselves before the Lord.

Amp Gal 6:7 Do not be deceived and deluded and misled; <u>God will not allow Himself to be sneered at (scorned, disdained, or mocked by mere pretensions or professions,</u> or by His precepts being set aside.) [He inevitably deludes himself who attempts to delude God.] For whatever a man sows, that and that only is what he will reap.

Amp Gal 6:8 For he who sows to his own flesh (lower nature, sensuality) will from the flesh reap decay and ruin and destruction, but <u>he who sows to the Spirit will from the Spirit reap eternal life.</u>

Amp Gal 6:9 And let us not lose heart and grow weary and faint in acting nobly and doing right, for in due time and at the appointed season we shall reap, if we do not loosen and relax our courage and faint.

For those believers who are Christians by pretense and profession only (of which the majority are when that time comes), they will have to endure the great tribulation. However, if they do not worship the beast, take his mark, or come off their testimony of Christ, they will be restored and join the ranks of heaven on the day of the first resurrection.

However, the pope/false prophet will attempt to force everyone, even the church he is the Holy See of, to bow down to the risen beast. In the end, when it is too late, he will show himself a tyrant and a fraud, lusting power with selfish ambition just as Saddam Hussein showed himself to be. Both wanting to raise Babylon beyond its glory of the past.

WEB Rev 13: 16 He (the false prophet) *causes all, the small and the great, the rich and the poor, and the free and the slave, to be given marks on their right hands, or on their foreheads; 17 and that no one would be able to buy or to sell, unless he has that mark, the name of the beast or the number of his name.*

The false prophet takes full advantage of his success in bringing the beast back to life and his killing of the two witnesses. He then orders everyone in the earth to take a mark signifying submission to the risen Nimrod, forcing everyone to worship him, and to denounce the God of the Christians and Jews. If they refuse, they die.

The globe is divided and given over to ten kings or world leaders who worship and serve the beast. Global domination is achieved! The ten kings likewise secure the newly formed global kingdom of the beast now void of God and His presence by immediately and systematically killing every man, woman, and child who will not renounce God and instead worship the antichrist. The whole world is made to worship the one who came back from death, killed God's two witnesses, and caused God's Spirit and His *Church Pure* to depart the earth. When Nimrod first walked the earth thousands of years previously, he swore to overpower God and then rule the whole earth by his power. He finally has the appearance of having done so!

Note: The sixth, seventh, and eighth kingdoms of the beast, are not ones in opposition to each other, but ones which metamorphized into three different forms changing hands three different times. The sixth and seventh kingdom (or heads of the beast) have Rome as its center, or as it is called during that time, "the great city" of Babylon.

NIV Rev 17:9 . . . *The seven heads are seven hills* (the Vatican City in Rome) *on which the woman sits.*

NIV Rev 17:18 The woman you saw is the great city that rules over the kings of the earth."

This verse 18 means the woman, the *Church Corrupt*, becomes the seventh kingdom of the beast, which in reality is the revived Roman Empire. She no longer is just prostituting herself with the Roman Empire, the sixth kingdom of the beast, whose head/center was also in Rome. She becomes the great city of Babylon and rules the kings of the earth and she does it from Rome, the city on seven hills.

The seventh king and kingdom, the pope and the Vatican, bridges the sixth to the eighth by reviving the fatal head wound of the beast in two forms.

1. Bring back the former territories of the Roman Empire under the pope's control by uniting under himself the ten kings who rule the territories of the former Roman Empire. Them making their consolidation the Holy Roman Empire, keeping Rome as the "great city who rules the kings of the earth. All of which in turn becomes the seventh kingdom.

2. Bring back from the dead the first king of Babylon, Nimrod, to gain complete control of the entire world which becomes the eighth and only truly global kingdom of Nimrod's.

Each horn in the prophetic picture of the destiny of the beast out of the earth is the power God granted him as king and false prophet to accomplish the reviving of both, the Roman Empire and the beast himself. Finally, the eighth king, who is the risen first king Nimrod, makes Jerusalem his center. It is where he is brought back from the dead, and as such Jerusalem then becomes the great city of Babylon—the city from which the risen beast rules all the kings of the earth.

NRSV Rev 11:7 When they (the two witnesses) *have finished their testimony, the beast that comes up from the bottomless pit* (the Abyss in Hades, the realm of the dead) *will make war on them and conquer them and kill them, 8 and their dead bodies will lie in the street of the great city that is prophetically called Sodom and Egypt, where also their Lord was crucified.*

The great city, which is always the center of the kingdom of Babylon who rules the kings of the earth, makes this move from Rome to Jerusalem fulfilling the prophecy which states:

Mic 5:5 And this One (Jesus) *will be our peace when the Assyrian invades our land and marches through our fortresses. We will raise against him seven shepherds, even eight leaders of men.*

Mic 5:6 *They will rule the land of Assyria with the sword, the land of Nimrod with drawn* *sword.* *He* *(Jesus)* *will deliver us* *from the Assyrian* *(the risen Nimrod and antichrist)* *when he invades our land and marches into our borders.*

One of the horns of power like a lamb given to the beast out of the earth is his destiny to be the seventh shepherd/king of the seventh kingdom. The horns of a lamb are small, and have a set time—one cycle of time which is a year. Although the pope attains authority over all the ten kingdoms (minus three) of the Roman Empire which he revived, he himself is king over a very little amount of territory. Mostly the territories of central Italy which, in time, shrinks down to the Vatican City, in Rome.

As for his second horn of power he is the false prophet and trusted minister of the kingdom of the risen Nimrod (who he also revived from the dead). It also is a small horn of power. By this horn of power he performs miracles on behalf of the antichrist, organizes the entire world as a single kingdom of the beast and does so again by creating ten sovereignties or horns of power. But this horn of power like a lamb is small because it will only last a single cycle, seven years, which is the hour of power given to the beast. Again, he will have a spiritual authority of sorts over the kings of the world being the minster of the beast but himself will be sovereign over very little.

It says about the beast who comes out of the earth/false prophet that he spoke like a dragon and has horns like a lamb. This is confirmed in Daniel connecting the two together as the same individual. In Daniel it said:

NIV Da 7:7 *"After that, in my vision at night I looked, and there before me was a fourth beast—* *terrifying and frightening and very powerful. It had large iron teeth; it crushed and devoured* *its victims and trampled underfoot whatever was left.* *It was different from all the former* *beasts, and it had ten horns.*
NIV Da 7:8 *"While I was thinking about the horns,* *there before me was another horn, a little one,* *which came up among them; and three of the first horns were uprooted before it.* *This horn* *had eyes like the eyes of a man and a mouth that spoke boastfully.*

Revelation: "(he) has horns like a lamb." Again, the horns of a lamb are small and only last for one cycle. As for the horns on the beast who come out of the sea, one is as the king of the seventh kingdom of the beast. The second horn is as the false prophet and minister of the beast.

Daniel: "While I was thinking about the horns, there before me was <u>another horn, a little one,</u> which came up among them. . ." this single little horn is one of the horns of power granted the false prophet.

Revelation: Verse 16:13 of Revelation calls the beast out of the earth, "the false prophet."

Daniel: "This horn had eyes like the eyes of a man . . ." A horn having eyes interprets as an individual who has spiritual sight—a prophet and spiritual leader. Once Daniel's prophecy is fulfilled, that horn of power which comes and who before three horns of the ten are uprooted, is revealed by history as the pope of the Roman Catholic Church who revives the Roman Empire. The Holy See (the pope) of the Roman Church is a prophet by definition.

Revelation: ". . . he spoke like a dragon . . ." He spoke like a devil it could say, seeing how the dragon/serpent is the Devil and Satan (Rev 12:9). The dragon is the Devil who is prideful, vain, and elevates himself above God and is seductive. As such, this does not simply mean he spoke ferociously. No, he spoke as the great seducer, the serpent. His words seduced, and intimidated. His words were boastful in that he falsely claimed an authority above authorities and the ten kings believed. The pope revived the fallen empire, making it under his own authority over the ten kingdoms who had the strength and defeated the Roman Empire. Indeed, he spoke like a dragon.

Daniel: [He had] a mouth that spoke boastfully. It says about the little horn in Daniel that it had a mouth which spoke boastfully. It was not by the might of an army, but by his boastful and arrogant manner and through deceit that Pope Leo III filled the void of power left by the Roman Empire. He took the broken pieces the ten kings consumed, unified them while making himself in authority over them by elevating his position as pope over them. He did all this without a shot fired!

As stated before, the false prophet uses the hatred of the two witnesses by the people of the earth and the *Church Corrupt.* He will rally them into letting him go into the temple, perform magic and create a body for Nimrod to come back to life with. All under the promise that he will save them from the torment of the two witnesses.

The false prophet is granted by God the power to bring to life Nimrod in the Frankenstein like body he creates for him. In trying to save themselves from the torment of the two witnesses, the people of the earth got much more than they bargained for in agreeing to bring back from the dead this monster who no one can stop or defend against.

> WEB Rev 13:18 *Here is wisdom. He who has understanding, let him calculate the number of the beast, for it is the number of a man. His number is six hundred sixty-six.*

Verse 18 above is verifying that the first beast having a prophetic picture of his destiny that shows him coming out of the sea with seven heads and ten horns is a person, an individual man. This is the case because it says that he has the number of a man, 666. These giants, including Nimrod, were demigods in that their fathers were angelic beings (or gods) and their mothers were mortal humans. However, in Genesis, God decides to call these giants who are half-celestial beings, mortal men. His reason He says in Genesis is because in the end they are clothed with flesh and die as all flesh dies. That is unlike the celestial fathers who spawned them, their celestial bodies are not subject to death.

Nimrod is purported as:
1) a giant
2) is recorded to be 2/3 god/celestial and 1/3 man
3) is the founder and first king of Babylon
4) comes back from the realm of the dead to walk the earth again
5) is able to kill the unkillable, the two witnesses
6) cannot be defeated in battle and is impossible to be killed by human hands (only because he must be killed the second time by being thrown alive into the lake of fire)

Considering all that it says above about Nimrod, the whole world from the beginning of man, both alive and dead, will be astonished. They will be in awe of him (that is except the elect who are written in the lambs book of life who have this knowledge prophetically). However, here we are told Nimrod is the founder of Babylon who boasts that he can kill God and comes back from the dead, but is just a man of flesh who dies and goes to the lake of fire. It is an inflated, vain pride which makes him so self important. He is only a man who is subject to death and is no match for the God who created all men and angels.

NIV Ps 2:1 *Why do the nations conspire and the peoples plot in vain?*

NIV Ps 2:2 *The kings of the earth take their stand and the rulers gather together against the LORD and against his Anointed One.*

NIV Ps 2:3 *"Let us break their chains," they say, "and throw off their fetters."*

NIV Ps 2:4 *The One enthroned in heaven laughs; the Lord scoffs at them.*

NIV Ps 2:5 *Then he rebukes them in his anger and terrifies them in his wrath, saying,*

NIV Ps 2:6 *"I have installed my King on Zion, my holy hill."*

NIV Ps 2:7 *I will proclaim the decree of the LORD: He said to me, "You are my Son; today I have become your Father.*

NIV Ps 2:8 *Ask of me, and I will make the nations your inheritance, the ends of the earth your possession.*

NIV Ps 2:9 *You will rule them with an iron scepter; you will dash them to pieces like pottery."*

NIV Ps 2:10 *Therefore, you kings, be wise; be warned, you rulers of the earth.*

NIV Ps 2:11 *Serve the LORD with fear and rejoice with trembling.*

NIV Ps 2:12 *Kiss the Son, lest he be angry and you be destroyed in your way, for his wrath can flare up in a moment. Blessed are all who take refuge in him.*

It is important to remember the relationship that numbers have with the Hebrew alphabet. Since the Hebrews do not have a separate set of symbols to represent numbers, the letters of the alphabet double as numbers too. Each letter has a numeric value and meaning.

That being the case, the Hebrews had (for the lack of a better word) a game or exercise in which they would add up the numeric values of each letter in a person's name, and whatever that number was, they would tell a person that number. It was then up to the person they told the number to, to figure out whose name it was, by using letters whose numeric values added up to the number given them. In this case, it is 666. To know the alpha letters whose values add up to 666, one would need to figure out the Hebrew translation and spelling of the name. This would render it next to impossible to decipher the number 666 into a name when there are multiple names given him. In fact, in order to not bring glory to this person in recorded history, the writer of Genesis did not use his real name but named him after his evil. Nimrod means the rebel or the one who causes the people to rebel.

However, even though it would be difficult to decode the number 666 into an alpha name in this day and age, the Bible already tells us through many different Scriptures, the identity of this individual who is identified by the number 666. It is Nimrod, grandson of Ham, who in the Bible and other documents have many different names he is called by. Perhaps John is telling us that it is the name he goes by when he rises from the dead in the future that will add up numerically as 666.

Nevertheless, the important thing is that this second narrative ends its telling of the main characters who are of the line of the offspring of the Devil with the profile of the false prophet, the beast who comes out of the earth. Revelation ends its telling of this line with saying the beast who seduces so many away from God, brings on the second judgment and is considered a god for doing so. However, he is merely a mortal man. He has the number of man, 666. Isaiah prophesies this about this man:

NIV Isa 14:9 *The grave below is all astir to meet you at your coming; it rouses the spirits of the departed to greet you—all those who were leaders in the world; it makes them rise from their thrones—all those who were kings over the nations.*
NIV Isa 14:10 *They will all respond, they will say to you, "You also have become weak, as we are; you have become like us."*
NIV Isa 14:11 *All your pomp has been brought down to the grave, along with the noise of your harps; maggots are spread out beneath you and worms cover you.*
NIV Isa 14:12 *How you have fallen from heaven, O morning star, son of the dawn! You have been cast down to the earth, you who once laid low the nations!*

The morning star is the sun. Nimrod started the cult worship of the sun and eventually was proclaimed to be the sun god. Here Isaiah mocks Nimrod as the sun that has fallen from the heavens or the morning sun which has turned to night and darkness after having just a short time to light the earth.

NIV Isa 14:12 ... *You have been cast down to the earth, you who once laid low the nations!*
NIV Isa 14:13 *You said in your heart, "I will ascend to heaven; I will raise my throne above the stars of God; I will sit enthroned on the mount of assembly, on the utmost heights of the sacred mountain.*
NIV Isa 14:14 *I will ascend above the tops of the clouds; I will make myself like the Most High."*
NIV Isa 14:15 *But you are brought down to the grave, to the depths of the pit.*
NIV Isa 14:16 *Those who see you stare at you, they ponder your fate: "Is this the man who shook the earth and made kingdoms tremble,*
NIV Isa 14:17 *the man who made the world a desert, who overthrew its cities and would not let his captives go home?"*
NIV Isa 14:18 *All the kings of the nations lie in state, each in his own tomb.*
NIV Isa 14:19a *But you are cast out of your tomb like a rejected branch;*

Nimrod being cast out of his tomb like a rejected branch is reference to when he comes back from the dead by the magic of the false prophet.

NIV Isa 14:19b *you are covered with the slain, with those pierced by the sword, those who descend to the stones of the pit. Like a corpse trampled underfoot,*
NIV Isa 14:20a *you will not join them in burial, for you have destroyed your land and killed your people.*

The slain pierced by the sword is reference to Nimrod's army who all die at the battle of Armageddon. However, when it says that he will not join them in the grave (burial) it is because he does not die in that battle against the Lord. Nor does he go to Hades where his dead and disembodied army goes. He has already had his time in the Abyss in Hades. Instead, he is thrown alive into the lake of fire 1,000 years before anyone else is cast into it.

NIV Isa 14:20b *The offspring of the wicked will never be mentioned again.*
NIV Isa 14:21 *Prepare a place to slaughter his sons for the sins of their forefathers; they are not to rise to inherit the land and cover the earth with their cities.*

"Prepare a place to slaughter his sons" That place is at the battle of Armageddon. "His sons for the sins of their forefathers" The line of offspring of the Devil will not rise to inherit the land. This place which is to be prepared is the lake of fire. All in Hades will rise from the dead, some to everlasting life, and some to the lake of fire.

NIV Isa 14:22 *"I will rise up against them," declares the LORD Almighty. "I will cut off from Babylon her name and survivors, her offspring and descendants," declares the LORD.*
NIV Isa 14:23 *"I will turn her into a place for owls and into swampland; I will sweep her with the broom of destruction," declares the LORD Almighty.*

The Lord will do so through the seven years of wrath, 3-1/2 years of discipline against Babylon in the Church, and 3-1/2 years of punishment against Babylon in the world. Never will it have a chance to rise again.

Notes

[2] *Roman Catholic Ten Commandments.* (2018, January 13). Retrieved April 2018, from The Ten Commandments: http://www.the-ten-commandments.org/romancatholic-tencommandments.html

CHAPTER 5

The Lamb and the 144,000

Now the narrative turns back towards the line of offspring of the woman clothed with the sun. This profile tells of the relationship between the 144,000 and the child the woman gave birth to. The 144,000 we have already learned are 12,000 from every tribe of Israel. That is the twelve tribes which are reflected as the twelve stars in the crown of the woman clothed with the sun.

Note: The prophetic profile or the prophetic picture worth a thousand words of Jesus shows Him here as a Lamb. However, previously, in the profile of the prophetic picture worth a thousand words of the woman clothed with the sun, Jesus is characterized simply as the child of the woman. Here is a good opportunity to understand how Revelation prophecy is outlined in a way that would easily escape notice. That is because of how obvious the identity of the child of the woman clothed with the sun is. Likewise, how obvious the identity of who the Lamb is. Both are Jesus! Later in Revelation Jesus is referred to as an angel or "messenger" which is not so obvious. Why an additional characterization? Because it is a second prophetic profile of Jesus which reveals a different aspect of His role or power as a main character. However, considering how easy it is to interpret the identity of the child and the Lamb and to relate the two as the same individual, it is good to pause and take note so that the other prophetic profiles of the main characters can more easily be interpreted.

Let's compare: Jesus was described as a child in the prophetic profile of the woman clothed with the sun. However, in His profile, His prophetic picture worth a thousand words, He is pictured as a Lamb. In the profile and prophetic picture of the seventh king of the empire of Babylon/pope of the Catholic Church, that individual is characterized as a beast—a beast who comes up out of the earth with two small horns, no less. However, later in Revelation when speaking about him outside his prophetic picture worth a thousand words, this seventh king and evil pope is referred to as the false prophet.

Knowing the literary style of visions in Revelation and how they are outlined by looking at one occasion, makes it easier to interpret and relate the different occasions. Especially when one individual is referred to with different pictures of him on different occasions. Likewise, while finding interpretation of Revelation, we can keep in mind that these profiles of the main characters are indeed prophetic characterizations which reveal the true nature of their hearts, and the ordained powers God has granted them which determine their destiny.

Rev 14:1a *I saw, and behold, the Lamb <u>standing on Mount Zion</u>, . . .*

As stated in the introduction(above), this next part is another prophetic profile of one of the main characters. It is the Lamb. The Lamb is Jesus, and He is standing on Mount Zion. Why a Lamb, and why on Mount Zion? This picture is telling us that Jesus has just finished sacrificing Himself like a lamb would be sacrificed as a sin offering. The fact that this setting shows that He has just completed His incredible act which reconciles man to God is very significant, as we will see in the verses to come. In addition, this picture tells us where on the timeline we are. What this tells us is that the significance of the 144,000 is here at this moment when Jesus had immediately finished His redeeming work on the cross, and not in the future.

Rev 14:1b *. . . and with him a number, one hundred forty-four thousand, having <u>his name, and the name of his Father, written on their foreheads</u>.*

Present with Jesus at this moment of the completion of His redeeming work and triumph, are the 144,000 who have been marked as God's. We originally learned about these 144,000 in the first narrative about the seven seals of Revelation. In that narrative they are called the "bondservants of God" and have been sealed as such by a mark of God on their foreheads. Likewise, it told us that their numbers consist of 12,000 from each of the 12 tribes of Israel.

The first narrative informed us that the second judgment of God, which began with the opening of the first four seals released the four horsemen. These four horsemen could not work their havoc on humanity until these 144,000 were marked as bondservants of God. Let us take note here that they were marked after the release of the four horsemen, and long before Jacob had twelve sons, even before those twelve sons had opportunity to give birth to 12,000 of each of them. How is it possible that they were marked as God's before the release of the four horsemen and before they were even born?

NLT Eph 1:3 *How we praise God, the Father of our Lord Jesus Christ, who has blessed us with every spiritual blessing in the heavenly realms because we belong to Christ.*
NLT Eph 1:4 <u>*Long ago, even before he made the world, God loved us and chose us in Christ to be holy and without fault in his eyes.*</u>
NLT Eph 1:5 *His unchanging plan has always been to adopt us into his own family by bringing us to himself through Jesus Christ. And this gave him great pleasure.*
NLT Eph 1:6 *So we praise God for the wonderful kindness he has poured out on us because we belong to his dearly loved Son.*

The answer is He knew us even before we were born. Our hearts were created in His heart even before we had a physical body.

> *Rev 14:2* *I heard a sound from heaven, like the sound of many waters, and like the sound of a great thunder. The sound which I heard was like that of harpists playing on their harps. 3 They sing a new song before the throne, and before the four living creatures and the elders. No one could learn the song except the one hundred forty-four thousand, <u>those who had been redeemed out of the earth.</u>*

These 144,000 along with all of heaven were in celebration because of what Jesus had just finished doing which made Him the Lamb. The 144,000 are seen before the four living creatures and the 24 elders which means they are before the throne of God! Since the first man (Adam) and because all men die becoming disembodied souls, no man could be before the throne of God. The disembodied are held over in Hades, the realm of the dead, even if it is in Abraham's bosom (the paradisiacal place in Hades), they all are separated from God until Jesus' sacrifice reconciles them to the Father. But because of what Jesus accomplished, these 144,000 are clothed in celestial bodies and become fit to stand before the throne of God in heaven. Could there be any cause for celebration in all of eternity greater than this; when Jesus succeeded in setting the dead free by giving His life in the body?

God created in Abel a new line of offspring from the woman clothed with the sun. This is after her sin corrupted the human spirit making her children the offspring of the Devil, possessing his corrupted spirit. Through that one person, righteous Abel, God was setting apart for Himself an entire line of offspring which would bring salvation through the "child" to come to the otherwise doomed human race. However, the Devil tried to eliminate that new line by having Cain kill Abel.

God gave Eve Seth to take the place of Abel and to keep His promise of the new line of offspring that would salvage the human race. From Seth to Noah there were many holy and righteous men. However, some 2,200 years after Seth, all in his line had also been corrupted by the ways of Cain. That is except the man Noah (Gen 6:8). It was one man, Noah, who God gave man a new beginning through. We all can trace our lineage back to Noah.

Through Noah's son, Shem, came Abraham. Through Abraham's grandson, Jacob, came his twelve sons who became the twelve tribes of Israel (Jacob was renamed Israel). These twelve tribes are the destiny and legacy of Eve and are represented in the prophetic characterization of her, by the crown of twelve stars on her head. Over time and out of each of those twelve tribes comes 12,000.

> *Rev 14:4a These are those who were not defiled with women, for they are (as) virgins. These are those who follow the Lamb wherever he goes.*

"These are those who follow the Lamb wherever He goes," is stating their new status as celestial humans having been redeemed. Just as we will do when we become celestial humans, they are with Jesus wherever He goes for all of eternity.

These 144,000 men go all the way back to Seth, making their genetics pure. They are not mixed with the genetics of giants or with any other way man's DNA has been corrupted. They are from the line of offspring of Eve. Out of the 144,000 comes the Christ who was promised would come out of Eve's legacy and be produced through her line of offspring.

Without this line of offspring who kept their genetics pure as Noah did back to Seth, it is questionable whether or not Jesus would have been able to come in the flesh and be the Son of Man. His flesh had to be what His Father made in Adam and Eve. It could not be the corrupted version which was mixed with celestial beings and their giants and animals in some cases, infecting man's DNA with every genetic deformity that has plagued man through the ages up to now. Yes, it is the genetic experiments in the times of antiquity which introduced imperfections into the human gene-pool, causing all kinds of handicaps and deformities.

Before the flood it was said that except Noah all flesh had become corrupt (Gen 6). However, from Noah through Shem leading up to the 144,000 there was a foundation of people who had uncorrupted genetics from which Jesus was born. In regards to His Spirit, it was pure and uncorrupted because as it is said, "what is conceived in Mary is from the Holy Spirit (Mat 1:20)."

Unlike all humans who possess the human spirit which was corrupted by the Devil, Jesus' Father is God, and He was conceived and born with the Spirit of His Father. He is the Son of Man in that through Mary (Eve), He had a body of flesh. He is the Son of God in that God impregnated Mary. Therefore, Jesus has God's Spirit as His own!

Jesus is the child Eve was promised which would come from her ordained destiny from God given her in the garden. Likewise, it is her child who will crush the head of both the Devil and his offspring who strike His heal. Indeed, these 144,000 are special to Jesus, as well as Israel from which they came. They are the people set apart for His purposes, and the redeeming line of offspring decreed by God to have come out of Eve.

> WEB Rev 14:4b *These were redeemed by Jesus from among men, the first fruits to God and to the Lamb.* 5 *In their mouth was found no lie, for they are blameless.*

There are all kinds of ideas who these 144,000 are or will be. But let's look at these verses 1-4 for what it says so we may know. They are with Jesus on Mount Zion the moment He accomplishes His sacrificial work on the cross which opened the door for man to be reconciled with God. Verse 4 (above) tells us they were redeemed as the first fruits of Jesus' work—first to be rescued from death (to be disembodied—a naked soul).

Let's put this together:

Rev 14:3 the one hundred forty-four thousand, those who had been redeemed out of the earth . . .

Rev 14:4b: These were redeemed by Jesus from among men, the first fruits to God and to the Lamb.

Verse 3 identifies the 144,000 as those who have been redeemed out of the earth. Verse 4b adds to their identity that they were the first to be redeemed from among men, "the first fruits."

We are told Jesus spent 3 days in Hades just as Jonah spent 3 days in the whale. While He was there, He set the prisoners free, the 144,000. We know this because we are told they are the first fruits to be redeemed.

NLT 1Pe 4:6 That is why the Good News was preached even to those who have died—so that although their bodies were punished with death, they could still live in the spirit as God does.

Then we are told in the Gospel of Matthew:

NIV Mt 27:50 And when Jesus had cried out again in a loud voice, he gave up his spirit.
NIV Mt 27:51 At that moment the curtain of the temple was torn in two from top to bottom. The earth shook and the rocks split.
NIV Mt 27:52 The tombs broke open and the bodies of many holy people who had died were raised to life.
NIV Mt 27:53 They came out of the tombs, and after Jesus' resurrection they went into the holy city and appeared to many people.

If the 144,000 are the first fruits who were able to be in the presence of the Father and clothed with a celestial body, then they are indeed the very first humans that were a product of the work Jesus did at the cross. The 144,000 are the first fruits and have already been redeemed. The breaking of the fifth seal recorded in the first narrative verifies and witnesses to this. The next person who could be counted among the numbers of celestial humans was Stephen, the first recorded follower of Christ to die. Although Eve had doomed all of humanity, in His judgment in the

Garden, God made a way that the legacy of Eve, the mother of all the living, could be salvaged and not entirely doomed. It was through this line of offspring, these 144,000 and those who kept themselves pure before them, going back to Seth, that God could come and be with us (Emanuel), bringing His salvation.

So when it says that the Lamb was on Mount Zion with the 144,000, we have to understand that we are seeing:

1) Jesus after His death in His resurrected body (celestial body).

2) With Him are the 144,000 souls after they had died and were rescued as a consequence of the cross. They too are with Him in their resurrected (celestial) bodies.

This is the prophetic picture that we are given concerning the Lamb and the 144,000. As a result of this prophetic picture, we can know:

- the time is after Jesus died on the cross
- the results of His work
- and the proof; the first fruits, the 144,000 who were the first to be redeemed as a result of Jesus' sacrifice.

This is the greatest and most wonderful picture in the history of history! It is the point of the whole story from the Garden, until the end! It is the plan that had seven seals on it that the Father gave the Son. The Son has not only revealed it to us, but has carried it out.

CHAPTER 6

The Three Angels

The three angels are the next of the profiles which give us a prophetic characterization, or a prophetic picture worth a thousand words of the main characters of Revelation, as listed in this second narrative. However, the third and next narrative of Revelation will begin with a prophetic characterization, or a prophetic picture worth a thousand words of the *Church Corrupt*. Nevertheless, this second narrative has given us prophetic profiles from both lines of offspring. Three from the Devil and his line of offspring, and seven from Eve and her line of offspring. The profiles start with Eve's and they end with profiles from her line of offspring. The Devil and his line of offspring is something that happens in the middle. They are as listed below:

1. Eve and her legacy (Israel - 144,000 - the Christ)
2. Devil and his line of offspring (the beast out of the sea and his seven kingdoms)
3. The beast out of the sea and his legacy (the seven kings and kingdoms, and ten kings who rule the world)
4. The second beast out of the earth (the false prophet)
5. The 144,000 (the first fruits of salvation)
6. The Christ (the child of the woman clothed with the sun)
7. The first of the two witnesses
8. The second of the two witnesses
9. The *Church Pure* and their fate
10. The *Church Corrupt* and their fate

To begin, the next three profiles are individuals who are characterized as angels. That is the best characterization of them that could be given. Angel (or the Hebrew and Greek words we translate as angel) actually means "messenger." According to its definition, it could be a human or a celestial being such as John the Baptist or Gabriel the angel, but an angel by definition is a messenger. In general, we use the term to describe a class of celestial beings who do the bidding of God. However, an angel is a messenger, and in either case these three individuals are best pictured as messengers who do the bidding of God.

The three messengers/angels in these prophetic profiles are Jesus the Christ, and the two witnesses. Along with the prophetic characterizations of them, there is given a description of their messages, in a nut shell.

> WEB Rev 14:6 *I saw an angel flying in mid heaven, having an eternal Good News to proclaim to those who dwell on the earth, and to every nation, tribe, language, and people. ⁷ He said with a loud voice, "Fear the Lord, and give him glory; for the hour of his judgment has come. Worship him who made the heaven, the earth, the sea, and the springs of waters!"*

"I saw an angel flying in the mid heavens (the sky) . . . (v. 6)", "a second angel followed . . . (v. 8)", "a third angel followed them . . . (v. 9)" is a great and accurate characterization! These words conjure up an image of these messengers as coming straight from God in heaven, flying down to the earth to give the message God had given them to tell the people of the earth.

Rev 10:1-2 in the first narrative describes this same messenger (Jesus) as an angel just as verse 6 above does:

NIV Rev 10:1 *Then I saw another mighty angel coming down from heaven. He was robed in a cloud, with a rainbow above his head; his face was like the sun, and his legs were like fiery pillars.*
NIV Rev 10:2 *He was holding a little scroll, which lay open in his hand. He planted his right foot on the sea and his left foot on the land,*
NIV Rev 10:3 *and he gave a loud shout like the roar of a lion. When he shouted, the voices of the seven thunders spoke.*

"I saw another mighty angel coming down from heaven . . . " If we were to understand that as saying; "I saw a mighty messenger coming down from heaven. He was robed in a cloud, with a rainbow above his head; his face was like the sun, and his legs were like fiery pillars . . . " could we believe anything other than this is describing the Lord Himself?

These two different verses (14:6 & 10:1-3) in which one is given in the first narrative and the other in the second, are speaking of the same individual and the same event, giving the same message. It is important to expound on these because they will become very interesting, especially the sequence of it all! Verse 10:2 from the first narrative tells us that, "He (Jesus) was holding a little scroll, which lay open in his hand." Verse 14:6 from the second narrative tells us Jesus is a messenger that comes directly from God with "an eternal Good News (the Gospel) to proclaim to those who dwell on the earth, and to every nation, tribe, language, and people." By this we know what that "laid open scroll contains is the "eternal Good News" that He got directly from God to give to us.

The book of Revelation begins with this opening statement:

NIV Rev 1:1 *The revelation of Jesus Christ, which God gave him to show his servants what must soon take place.*

The book of Revelation is the revelation (or testimony or message) of Jesus Christ, it says. God entrusting Jesus with this message to us, His servants, makes Jesus by definition an angel—a messenger. That revelation is prophecy about the future of mankind because it says that revelation of Jesus' is, "what must take place soon"— what must take place in the future, in other words. To know and speak the future is by definition, prophecy. The opening statement also makes it clear that it is God who gives Jesus this revelation with the purpose to share with us, His servants.

Next, it says:

Amp Rev 19:10 *. . . For the substance (essence) of the truth revealed by Jesus is the spirit of all prophecy [the vital breath, the inspiration of all inspired preaching and interpretation of the divine will and purpose, including both mine and yours].*

More simply translated:

NIV Rev 19:10 ... *For the testimony of Jesus is the spirit of prophecy."*

What this informs us of is that every prophet who has ever uttered a word from God in the history of mankind has done so by the Spirit of Jesus. Likewise, the words the prophets speak are from God given first to Jesus, then made known to His prophets by Jesus' Spirit—the Spirit of prophecy, then from the prophets who speaks them to us.

The next thing to look at is that John is taken to heaven before the throne of God and witnesses Him taking His place on His throne. Gathered around the throne are the 24 elders and the four living creatures. With a scroll sealed with seven seals in God's right hand, He takes His place in court. Then we are told:

NIV Rev 5:2 ... *I saw a mighty angel proclaiming in a loud voice, "Who is worthy to break the seals and open the scroll?"*
NIV Rev 5:3 But <u>no one in heaven or on earth or under the earth could open the scroll or even look inside it.</u>
NIV Rev 5:4 *I wept and wept because no one was found who was worthy to open the scroll or look inside.*
NIV Rev 5:5 <u>Then one of the elders said to me, "Do not weep! See, the Lion of the tribe of Judah, the Root of David, has triumphed. He is able to open the scroll and its seven seals."</u>

We are told that no one, dead or alive, in heaven or on earth knows what is in the scroll, or, for that matter can know, or is worthy to know. In fact, we are told in the beginning:

NIV Rev 5:6 *Then I saw a Lamb, looking as if it had been slain, standing in the center of the throne, encircled by the four living creatures and the elders. He had seven horns and seven eyes, which are the seven spirits of God sent out into all the earth.*
NIV Rev 5:7 <u>He came and took the scroll from the right hand of him who sat on the throne.</u>

NIV Rev 6:1 <u>I watched as the Lamb opened the first of the seven seals.</u>

A literal translation of verse 6 would say, "a Lamb looking as if its throat had been cut." Here is where the sequence of events in Revelation become interesting. At first glance we can understand by this that Jesus did His redeeming work already at this point, and because He did, it makes Him worthy to open the scroll. In support of this, John's vision of this event happened many years after he himself walked with Jesus during His ministry and also witnessed Jesus dying on the cross. However, verse 10:1 tells us:

NIV Rev 10:1 Then I saw another mighty angel (Jesus) coming down from heaven. He was robed in a cloud, with a rainbow above his head; his face was like the sun, and his legs were like fiery pillars.
NIV Rev 10:2 He was holding a little scroll, which lay open in his hand.

Verse 10:1-2 (above) is describing when Jesus came to the earth and began His ministry by telling us the Good News which is His testimony and is the revelation God gave Him in heaven. An important note is that the seals are broken and the scroll is opened. The content inside the scroll is what He came to tell the world.

NIV Rev 1:1 The revelation of Jesus Christ, which God gave him to show his servants what must soon take place.

Next to look at in this prophetic picture is that the scroll is opened and Jesus is revealing it to us before He died. It is when He went town to town with John and the other Apostles proclaiming that which God told Him to tell us—His testimony/revelation that the Father gave Him to give to us. A revelation that He had to die on the cross to show His worthiness of receiving this testimony.

It only stands to reason that Jesus had to know the contents of the scroll before He could tell us, thus the scroll is "laid open" in His hand. However, when Jesus received the scroll (sealed) from His Father in heaven, John saw Him pictured as the Lamb who already had His throat cut and had been sacrificed.

In real time how can that be? In one vision John is shown Jesus seemingly died first so that His worth was proven, then He received the scroll and was able to open it.

However, there were two more visions (10:1-3 and 14:6) that showed John that Jesus came to the earth having already opened the scroll and was delivering that message to us from the Father. In fact John walked with Jesus and witnessed when He did reveal the contents of the scroll to the people before He went to the cross.

Furthermore, to complicate things, it was Jesus, by His Spirit, who told all the prophets throughout history what they spoke to us, and what they recorded in the Bible. When pieced together, the prophets of old told us the entire story of what was sealed in the scroll. No one else could have told the prophets except Jesus, the Lord. Why? The book of Revelation tells us it is His revelation, His testimony, and He is the Spirit of prophecy. Finally, God told Him alone because no one else was found worthy.

Going back even further, Jesus the Lord, who is the Spirit of prophecy, told Adam, Eve, and the serpent in the Garden what will happen according to God's plan of judgment and redemption. That plan is part of the scroll's content, which had seven seals. That plan was not revealed to anyone until it was received by Jesus and revealed through Him. The most important factor that everything adds up to is that for God's prophets to have spoken, the scroll had to be revealed or opened by the Lord, before He spoke His decrees to Adam, Eve, and the serpent in the Garden! It had to be!

How can we reconcile this timeline conundrum? Here is the key:

NIV Rev 5:5 *Then one of the elders said to me, "Do not weep! See, the Lion of the tribe of Judah, the Root of David, has triumphed. He is able to open the scroll and its seven seals."*
NIV Rev 5:6 *Then I saw a Lamb, looking as if it had been slain, standing in the center of the throne, encircled by the four living creatures and the elders. He had seven horns and seven eyes, which are the seven spirits of God sent out into all the earth.*
NIV Rev 5:7 *He came and took the scroll from the right hand of him who sat on the throne.*

John was called up to heaven to see these visions. When Revelation began, it started with a mighty trumpet blast. Jesus and heaven came to John when he was in prayer. Behind him he could reach out and touch the feet of Jesus. However, after the seven letters were dictated, that porthole closed up and another opened. Before John could adjust from the one, another one opened. This time not behind John, but in front of him. The same voice called him up with a voice like a trumpet blast from behind a door saying, "come up here, and I will show you what must take place." John was brought up to heaven this time, and where he was taken was outside of time. He was given multiple visions which comprise the book of Revelation.

John was brought outside of time and was given a vision of when the Father presented to Jesus His plan for the final judgment and redemption of the human race. That is the scene of the opening of the seven seals. However, when no one was found worthy to open the scroll and thus have the responsibility of delivering this message to the people of the earth, John began to weep. However, keep in mind in real time that John had previously witnessed Jesus on earth and followed Him when He delivered that message.

Nevertheless, caught up in the intensity of the vision, and in his grief, one of the elders came to him and said:

NIV Rev 5:5 *Then one of the elders said to me, "Do not weep! See, the Lion of the tribe of Judah, the Root of David, has triumphed. He is able to open the scroll and its seven seals."*
NIV Rev 5:6 *Then I saw a Lamb, looking as if it had been slain, standing in the center of the throne, encircled by the four living creatures and the elders. He had seven horns and seven eyes, which are the seven spirits of God sent out into all the earth.*
NIV Rev 5:7 *He came and took the scroll from the right hand of him who sat on the throne.*

The elder said, "do not weep, see . . ." The elder, in his compassion to comfort John, gave him a vision within a vision. In that vision within a vision, John saw Jesus there receiving the scroll appearing as a lamb with its throat cut as if it had been sacrificed. Jesus, indeed, is not a lamb! Nor does His form look like a lamb! By Jesus having been pictured as a lamb with its throat cut, we know it was a vision, a visual representation of Jesus and not a real time sighting of Him.

John was within a vision already. The elder felt compassion for John because the reality of that vision had unglued him. However, before he got too hopeless and disturbed, the elder gave John this vision within a vision. He said to John, "do not weep, see . . ." In other words, "see" this vision so you know there is hope. As Jesus is being revealed to be worthy and was taking the scroll, He is pictured as a sacrificed lamb. It's as if that picture of Him being a lamb is being projected onto the true form of Jesus as He takes the scroll. Better yet, the vision allowed John to see past the outer form of Jesus and showed him a prophetic picture of His inner man. Just as seeing Eve as a woman clothed with the sun and having a crown of twelve stars on her head, John could see that in Jesus was that destiny and commitment to sacrifice Himself as a result of being the one who received the scroll.

When the elders said to John "see . . . (Jesus) has triumphed," it was for John to look at the vision to see how it is true. All the elder had to do was to ask John to behold the vision and say Jesus triumphed. Then for John to see that picture worth a thousand words it would tell John the rest of the story of what the elder wanted him to know. Then after viewing that picture of Jesus' destiny and commitment the elder said, "He is able to open the scroll and its seven seals." Meaning, now you know what gives Jesus the right, making Him worthy.

The objection to this interpretation would be that the elder did say, "See, the Lion of the tribe of Judah, the Root of David, has triumphed" before He opened the scroll. Putting the emphasis on "has" which means it had already happened. In real time it did already happen. In fact, John witnessed in his lifetime when His sacrifice happened. However, that changes nothing. John was taken out of time and was given a vision back in time of when the Father gave Jesus His plan of judgment and redemption. The giving of the scroll happed after original sin when the ark could be seen in the temple in heaven.

NIV Rev 11:19 Then the sanctuary of God in heaven was thrown open, and <u>the ark of His covenant was seen standing inside in His sanctuary</u>; and there were flashes of lightning, loud rumblings (blasts, mutterings), peals of thunder, an earthquake, and a terrific hailstorm.

It was then, after that sighting of Jesus (the ark) in the heavenly temple that the new destinies were given to the main characters of Revelation. It is during that sighting that the Lord received the scroll. It was during His reception of the scroll that His fate, destiny, and commitment now became one of a sacrifice in order to salvage man. It was after He opened it that the Lord confronted Adam, Eve, and the Devil in the Garden. It was when He decreed to them His judgment and redemption that their fates were sealed, their purposes and destinies were changed because of what they had done. It was that moment that was prophetically pictured for John to see the woman clothed with the sun and a crown of twelve stars, and the dragon with seven heads, seven crowns, and ten horns. These visions were their altered fates now that they had sinned.

Jesus explains to the people why He was worthy:

NLT Jn 10:2 *"I assure you, anyone who sneaks over the wall of a sheepfold, rather than going through the gate, must surely be a thief and a robber!*
NLT Jn 10:2 *For a shepherd enters through the gate.*
NLT Jn 10:3 *The gatekeeper opens the gate for him, and the sheep hear his voice and come to him. He calls his own sheep by name and leads them out.*
NLT Jn 10:4 *After he has gathered his own flock, he walks ahead of them, and they follow him because they recognize his voice.*
NLT Jn 10:5 *They won't follow a stranger; they will run from him because they don't recognize his voice."*
NLT Jn 10:6 *Those who heard Jesus use this illustration didn't understand what he meant,*
NLT Jn 10:7 *so he explained it to them. "I assure you, I am the gate for the sheep," he said.*
NLT Jn 10:8 *"All others who came before me were thieves and robbers. But the true sheep did not listen to them.*
NLT Jn 10:9 *Yes, I am the gate. Those who come in through me will be saved. Wherever they go, they will find green pastures.*
NLT Jn 10:10 *The thief's purpose is to steal and kill and destroy. My purpose is to give life in all its fullness.*
NLT Jn 10:11 *"I am the good shepherd. The good shepherd lays down his life for the sheep.*
NLT Jn 10:12 *A hired hand will run when he sees a wolf coming. He will leave the sheep because they aren't his and he isn't their shepherd. And so the wolf attacks them and scatters the flock.*
NLT Jn 10:13 *The hired hand runs away because he is merely hired and has no real concern for the sheep.*
NLT Jn 10:14 *"I am the good shepherd; I know my own sheep, and they know me,*
NLT Jn 10:15 *just as my Father knows me and I know the Father. And I lay down my life for the sheep.*

God wanted His people who would be redeemed to understand exactly what their hope was, what He was going to do, and why. He did not want His people to be in the dark but wanted them to know everything that was to happen. The elder could not sit there and watch John travail in his sorrow because no one was found worthy to open the scroll and make it their own testimony. Neither does God, the Creator of heaven and earth and of humanity, want us to have the sorrow of hopelessness as we are swept away with the destruction of all creation when He has made a way of redemption, a hope, and a future. From the very beginning in the Garden it has been the Lord, and the Lord alone, who has made sure His elect and line of offspring know exactly what His plans are and what will happen.

There is one thing which should never escape us about these three angels/messengers!

In the first narrative we learned in the second interlude between the sixth and seventh trumpet blast: That Jesus coming down to the earth to give His testimony and the two witnesses giving their testimonies, is the beginning and the end of the same message.

NIV Rev 5:6 Then I saw a Lamb, looking as if it had been slain, standing in the center of the throne . . .

NIV Rev 5:7 He came and took the scroll from the right hand of him who sat on the throne.

NLT Jn 10:15 just as my Father knows me and I know the Father. And I lay down my life for the sheep.

God needed someone who would give this message of judgment and redemption from the Father to a lost, hostile, violent, and Godless world, that watches out for number one at any cost. It was clear from the beginning that whoever He was, He would be rejected and killed in trying to proclaim that Good News. Whoever would take that scroll from the right hand of the Father and make it his testimony to give to the world, knew in advance that the world would be ungrateful and hostile towards it, they would not only reject the testimony and messenger, but kill Him.

The Lord's Suffering Servant

NLT Isa 52:13 *See, my servant will prosper; he will be highly exalted.*

NLT Isa 52:14 *Many were amazed when they saw him—beaten and bloodied, so disfigured one would scarcely know he was a person.*

NLT Isa 52:15 *And he will again startle many nations. Kings will stand speechless in his presence. For they will see what they had not previously been told about; they will understand what they had not heard about.*

NLT Isa 53:1 *Who has believed our message? To whom will the LORD reveal his saving power?*

NLT Isa 53:2 *My servant grew up in the Lord's presence like a tender green shoot, sprouting from a root in dry and sterile ground. There was nothing beautiful or majestic about his appearance, nothing to attract us to him.*

NLT Isa 53:3 *He was despised and rejected—a man of sorrows, acquainted with bitterest grief. We turned our backs on him and looked the other way when he went by. He was despised, and we did not care.*

NLT Isa 53:4 *Yet it was our weaknesses he carried; it was our sorrows that weighed him down. And we thought his troubles were a punishment from God for his own sins!*

NLT Isa 53:5 *But he was wounded and crushed for our sins. He was beaten that we might have peace. He was whipped, and we were healed!*

NLT Isa 53:6 *All of us have strayed away like sheep. We have left God's paths to follow our own. Yet the LORD laid on him the guilt and sins of us all.*

NLT Isa 53:7 *He was oppressed and treated harshly, yet he never said a word. He was led as a lamb to the slaughter. And as a sheep is silent before the shearers, he did not open his mouth.*

NLT Isa 53:8 *From prison and trial they led him away to his death. But who among the people realized that he was dying for their sins—that he was suffering their punishment?*

NLT Isa 53:9 *He had done no wrong, and he never deceived anyone. But he was buried like a criminal; he was put in a rich man's grave.*

NLT Isa 53:10 *But it was the Lord's good plan to crush him and fill him with grief. Yet when his life is made an offering for sin, he will have a multitude of children, many heirs. He will enjoy a long life, and the Lord's plan will prosper in his hands.*

NLT Isa 53:11 *When he sees all that is accomplished by his anguish, he will be satisfied. And because of what he has experienced, my righteous servant will make it possible for many to be counted righteous, for he will bear all their sins.*

NLT Isa 53:12 I will give him the honors of one who is mighty and great, because he exposed himself to death. He was counted among those who were sinners. He bore the sins of many and interceded for sinners.

Who would give themselves up for that? There was no one, not on earth alive or dead or in heaven. What would be the point? The messenger who would accept this testimony of the scroll with seven seals would gladly proclaim it and the world would not take heed but ungratefully kill them. In your torment and during your dying breath, one would not help but feel it was all for not, nobody believed at that point. Understanding all this before accepting the call to be that messenger, who would rise up?

NIV Ro 5:5 And hope does not disappoint us, because God has poured out his love into our hearts by the Holy Spirit, whom he has given us.
NIV Ro 5:6 You see, at just the right time, when we were still powerless, Christ died for the ungodly.
NIV Ro 5:7 Very rarely will anyone die for a righteous man, though for a good man someone might possibly dare to die.
NIV Ro 5:8 But God demonstrates his own love for us in this: While we were still sinners, Christ died for us.
NIV Ro 5:9 Since we have now been justified by his blood, how much more shall we be saved from God's wrath through him!
NIV Ro 5:10 For if, when we were God's enemies, we were reconciled to him through the death of his Son, how much more, having been reconciled, shall we be saved through his life!
NIV Ro 5:11 Not only is this so, but we also rejoice in God through our Lord Jesus Christ, through whom we have now received reconciliation.

Yes! It took the Lord Himself to do this thing that though judged for utter extinction already, this gift of redemption would cost His life to offer it.

As stated, these three angels are the beginning and end of the same message and same work. No one could kill the two witnesses. In the end, when their message was complete and the whole world rejected it, they killed them. However, God raised them to their feet 3-1/2 days later. Then God called them up to heaven to the fear and astonishment of the entire world. If no one could kill them and God had the power to raise them from the dead and lift them up to heaven as He did, then it must be asked, why? Why make these angels, these messengers with the Good News, suffer so and be killed when the power was there to not let it happen?

NIV Lk 14:21 *"The servant came back and reported this to his master. Then the owner of the house became angry and ordered his servant, 'Go out quickly into the streets and alleys of the town and bring in the poor, the crippled, the blind and the lame.'*

This (above) was the call of the Gentiles, it is the Church called after the Master was angry that the Jews would not take their place.

NIV Lk 14:22 *" 'Sir,' the servant said, 'what you ordered has been done, but there is still room.'*
NIV Lk 14:23 *"Then the master told his servant, 'Go out to the roads and country lanes and make them come in, so that my house will be full.*

The message of the two witnesses is not to the redeemed who would be raptured along with them to heaven—the *Church Pure*. It is to the *Church Corrupt*, it is to the great multitude who are the numbers beyond counting who will not listen to them until it is too late. They are those found on the roads and country lanes in the above parable. They are the ones who will rise up to meet Jesus at the first resurrection of the dead, exactly 3-1/2 years after the two witnesses have been called up. The two witnesses know they and their message will be met not with joy, but rejected with hostility.

The testimony of the two witnesses is for the people that they know will reject them. Their testimony tells them about what will happen after they leave. They tell them that although the Spirit of God will not be in the earth for 3-1/2 years all is not lost. If they do not take the mark of the beast, do not worship him, and do not give up their testimony of Christ, 3-1/2 years later they will rise to life and join Jesus in the sky for eternity.

Knowing they would not be believed, the two witnesses, these last two angels, let themselves be killed by the beast who will kill the great multitude. Then demonstrate after 3-1/2 days (each day representing a year), raise back to life and afterwards taken up in celestial bodies to join Jesus in the sky. They do just as Jesus had done! It is because they give up their lives to show to those who hate them that after it's too late, the people can remember what they were told by them and have witnessed with their own eyes, believe, and finally be saved.

We need only to look at the message the two witnesses speak as revealed in their profile (below) to know this to be true.

Before accepting their destiny from God, knowing their good deed will be met with rejection, hatred, hostility, and death, these two angels (messengers) still take that testimony and give witness with their very lives just as the first angel—Jesus— did before them. The two witnesses are the servants who as per instructed went out on the country roads to bring more into the house of the Lord. Because of their sacrifice, the Master's house will be filled up with them, the great multitude, at the first resurrection and before Jesus returns to rule the earth with His bride.

> *WEB Rev 14:8 Another, a second angel, followed, saying, "Babylon the great has fallen, which has made all the nations to drink of the wine of the wrath of her sexual immorality."*

This (above) is an announcement of the great tribulation and is referring to the *Church Corrupt.* The great tribulation begins when the two witnesses are caught up to heaven. In reality they give their testimony together. However, in this profile which gives a prophetic characterization of them, it divides up their message in this vision in order to accredit both of them with a portion of their testimony. Accordingly, below the second witness (the third angel) gives his message. He tells them how to endure the great tribulation and be saved.

> *WEB Rev 14:9 Another angel, a third, followed them, saying with a great voice, "If anyone worships the beast and his image, and receives a mark on his forehead, or on his hand, 10 he also will drink of the wine of the wrath of God, which is prepared unmixed in the cup of his anger. He will be tormented with fire and sulfur in the presence of the holy angels, and in the presence of the Lamb. 11 The smoke of their torment goes up forever and ever. They have no rest day and night, those who worship the beast and his image, and whoever receives the mark of his name.*

Their message is not one of evangelism but instruction for when they are gone, the rapture has transpired, and it is too late to avoid the things to come. Babylon and its seventh kingdom, the *Church Corrupt* will fall because of her sins and participation with the world. However, the third angel speaks that if you take these measures, you will not be lost in torment for all of eternity.

WEB Rev 14:12 *Here is the perseverance of the saints, those who keep the commandments of God, and the faith of Jesus." ¹³ I heard a voice from heaven saying, "Write, 'Blessed are the dead who die in the Lord from now on.'" "Yes," says the Spirit, "that they may rest from their labors; for their works follow with them."*

Their testimony is complete. They are rejected and killed, then raised from the dead and lifted with the *Church Pure* to heaven. Verse 12 (above) closes the prophetic profile of the three angels with a last word for those whose eyes are opened after they have gone. The fate of the *Church Corrupt* has been sealed and it will take endurance of the great tribulation to save them now. That is to endure them patiently in the way the two witnesses both instructed and demonstrated.

CHAPTER 7

The Harvest of the Earth

The next two prophetic pictures worth a thousand words are about the Church. They distinguish the *Church Pure* from the *Church Corrupt* as well as the fate of both. Although the fate or destination of both are the same, the way they get there are in stark contrast to each other. The wheat is the *Church Pure*, and the grapes are the *Church Corrupt.*

It is so amazing that the Lord tells the story of man again in this second narrative, however, He doesn't do so in a story form, as in a chronological listing of one event that follows after another. Instead the Lord gives individual profiles in the form of visions which have elements within them that represent everything we need to know about the subjects of the visions. This is most unlike the snapshot that photographs give which capture a moment in time.

These individual profiles are given in a way that they create a timeline by the order they are given, which in turn very clearly tells the story of man, past, present, and future. The story starts out with Eve (the woman clothed with the sun) and the Devil (the red dragon). Their profiles define the lineage of both of their lines of offspring. It likewise reveals the antagonism between the two of them (Eve and the Devil), and also between their two different lines of offspring. For Eve, it is Israel and the Savior. For the Devil, it is Babylon and the antichrist.

Next, the profiles bring us to the aftermath of the flood and the emergence of the antichrist (the beast out of the sea). Then, after him we are shown the profile of the false prophet (the beast out of the earth). The placement of this profile may, at first glance, seem like a leap forward breaking the timeline. However, since they are so closely tied together, the story of the antichrist cannot be made complete without the profile of the false prophet. Additionally, the future role and relationship the false prophet has with the antichrist is the same as back when Nimrod and Terrah walked the earth, a couple generations after the flood.

The role and spirit of the false prophet was first embodied by Terah, the father of Abraham. Terah led the people to worship Nimrod and the system of idols and gods he and Nimrod created. He did so to cause the people to rebel against the One God who created the heavens and the earth. Given this, the story of the false prophet indeed began with Terah back in the times of Nimrod, and is merely continued in the future when the great tribulation is upon us.

What follows is the 144,000 who come from the 12 tribes of Israel. The human gene-pool is kept pure and intact from Adam and Eve through their son Seth down to Noah. The rest of mankind corrupted the human DNA through the crossbreeding of natural humans with celestial beings before the flood. The importance of the corruption of human DNA cannot be overstated! Then after the flood from Noah, through his son Shem, came Abraham and the 12 tribes of Israel. Elements of every tribe of Israel kept themselves pure producing the 144,000. Out of them and because of their heart for the true God, the Christ was able to come and do His redeeming work.

The timeline turns to the three messengers of God (the three angels). They deliver that saving testimony to the people of the earth. First through the Christ, then concluding with the two witnesses. At the close of the Gospel being released, the two witness are snatch up, and the great tribulation begins. This is the moment the wheat and the grapes have their different paths in becoming the bride of Christ.

Finally, is the annihilation of Babylon. It starts with the destruction of Babylon in the Church (the grapes) and then the prophetic picture worth a thousand words comes to a conclusion with the sevenness of the destruction of Babylon. That includes the Devil's line of offspring in the world who are punished with the seven bowls of plagues.

WEB Rev 14:14 I looked, and behold, a white cloud; and on the cloud one sitting like a son of man, having on his head a golden crown, and in his hand a sharp sickle.

Amp Ac 1:9 And when He had said this, even as they were looking [at Him], <u>He was caught up, and a cloud received and carried Him away out of their sight.</u>

Amp Ac 1:10 And while they were gazing intently into heaven as He went, behold, two men [dressed] in white robes suddenly stood beside them,

Amp Ac 1:11 Who said, Men of Galilee, why do you stand gazing into heaven? <u>This same Jesus, Who was caught away and lifted up from among you into heaven, will return in [just] the same way in which you saw Him go into heaven.</u>

This angel/messenger who is "like a son of man," is Jesus. The last prophetic profile that included Jesus and the two witnesses finished with their message being given and completed. Now it is the time for the harvest of both the wheat and the grapes. The Gospel and the Church Age have come to their end and all are ripe for harvesting.

WEB Rev 14:15 Another angel came out of the temple, crying with a loud voice to him who sat on the cloud, "Send your sickle, and reap; for the hour to reap has come; for the harvest of the earth is ripe!"

This verse witnesses to what Jesus told His Disciples:

Amp Ac 1:7 He said to them, It is not for you to become acquainted with and know what time brings [the things and events of time and their definite periods] or fixed years and seasons (their critical niche in time), which the Father has appointed (fixed and reserved) by His own choice and authority and personal power.

NLT Mt 24:36 "However, no one knows the day or the hour when these things will happen, <u>not even the angels in heaven or the Son himself.</u> Only the Father knows.

Right before it is time for the harvest we find Jesus at the ready with a sickle in His hand! However, it took an angel who came directly from the Father who tells Jesus that now is the time to harvest. He waited and was in need of being informed of what only the Father knew just as He had told His disciples (above). Jesus went on to say the things below regarding this time and event of the wheat being harvested.

NLT Mt 24:37 *"When the Son of Man returns, it will be like it was in Noah's day.*

NLT Mt 24:38 *In those days before the Flood, the people were enjoying banquets and parties and weddings right up to the time Noah entered his boat.*

NLT Mt 24:39 *People didn't realize what was going to happen until the Flood came and swept them all away. That is the way it will be when the Son of Man comes.*

The people not realizing what was going to happen to them until the flood came and swept them all away, is the comparison Jesus is making about the arrival of the seven years of God's wrath being poured out on the world. 3-1/2 years of the great tribulation poured out on the *Church Corrupt* and 3-1/2 years of wrath against the world. Together these 7 years utterly destroy every trace of Babylon in the world. However, the first 3-1/2 years of the great tribulation is the harvest of the grapes (the *Church Corrupt*), as we will explore next. On the very onset of the day that the harvest of the grapes begins, the wheat is harvested with one fell swoop, with a catching up to heaven (the *Church Pure*)!

Righteous Lot and his family who did not agree with abusing the manifest angels, attempted to restrain the madness of the people of Sodom and Gomorrah. The people had wanted to create a giant by somehow mixing human DNA with that of the angels. They saw it as the answer to protect themselves. The world and the *Church Corrupt* led by the pope will want to bring back from the dead the giant Nimrod to protect themselves from the two witnesses. The *Church Corrupt* will not believe the two witnesses are representing God by all the condemning things they say against the people and the harshness of their signs and wonders.

This is due to the fact that the *Church Corrupt* is a church that gives acceptance without conformity. They have come to accept the sinner and his sin, and as a result bring a harmony to humanity—a "coexistence" philosophy, as it were. The two witnesses will vehemently rail against this trend of the whole world. And that is why they will hate the two witnesses and believe they are not from God.

The Lord was able to save righteous Lot and his family from the madness of the multitude and their plans. The entire population of these two city-states unanimously lusted after this plan. The world and the *Church Corrupt* are turning God into something of their own making—a God who gives acceptance without conformity. When the two witnesses attempt to wake the *Church Corrupt* from their disillusion, they will hate the two witnesses and want them to be killed rather than come into the truth.

They had turned God into a god who gives acceptance without conformity, and cannot believe that the good God doesn't forgive everyone. That decidedly is not the way of God as we learned in the story of Cain. However, it is the way of Nimrod who tells the people, "Do as you will and I will, protect you from Yahweh." Nimrod is the god who gives acceptance without conformity that the *Church Corrupt* is ignorantly worshipping. Jesus said in Daniel:

NIV Da 12:10 Many will be purified, made spotless and refined, but the wicked will continue to be wicked. None of the wicked will understand, but those who are wise will understand.
NIV Da 12:11 "From the time that the daily sacrifice is abolished (the midpoint of the last seven) *and the abomination that causes desolation is set up, there will be 1,290 days* (thirty days after the last seven is complete).
NIV Da 12:12 Blessed is the one who waits for and reaches the end of the 1,335 days

Just as the Lord saved Lot and his family from the sudden and utter destruction of Sodom and Gomorrah by evacuating them, on that 1,335th day after the sacrifices are ordered to stop, the Lord will likewise evacuate the *Church Pure*. The harvest of the wheat is that evacuation of the *Church Pure*. They will be caught up, or as some describe, "raptured." That day will have finally come in which Jesus said:

NIV Jn 14:18 I will not leave you as orphans; I will come to you.
NIV Jn 14:19 Before long, the world will not see me anymore, but you will see me. Because I live, you also will live.
NIV Jn 14:20 On that day you will realize that I am in my Father, and you are in me, and I am in you.
NIV Jn 14:21 Whoever has my commands and obeys them, he is the one who loves me. He who loves me will be loved by my Father, and I too will love him and show myself to him."

The *Church Pure*, those in *spiritual union* with Him, obeying every prompting of His Spirit inside them, will suddenly find themselves standing before Jesus and the Father clothed in a celestial body. Again, that is the harvest of the wheat.

WEB Rev 14:16 He who sat on the cloud thrust his sickle on the earth, and the earth was reaped.

NLT Mt 24:40 "Two men will be working together in the field; one will be taken, the other left.

NLT Mt 24:41 Two women will be grinding flour at the mill; one will be taken, the other left.

NLT Mt 24:42 So be prepared, because you don't know what day your Lord is coming.

NLT Mt 24:43 "Know this: A homeowner who knew exactly when a burglar was coming would stay alert and not permit the house to be broken into.

NLT Mt 24:44 You also must be ready all the time. For the Son of Man will come when least expected.

NLT Mt 24:45 "Who is a faithful, sensible servant, to whom the master can give the responsibility of managing his household and feeding his family?

NLT Mt 24:46 If the master returns and finds that the servant has done a good job, there will be a reward (they will be caught up).

NLT Mt 24:47 I assure you, the master will put that servant in charge of all he owns.

That "reward" will happen when Jesus returns and establishes His Kingdom here on earth. The celestial humans will live in the New Jerusalem with the Lord and rule the mortal humans on the earth. They will be put in charge of the Kingdom of the Lord, they will be kings and priests while ministering His rule.

WEB Rev 14:17 Another angel came out of the temple which is in heaven. He also had a sharp sickle. 18 Another angel came out from the altar, he who has power over fire, and he called with a great voice to him who had the sharp sickle, saying, "Send your sharp sickle, and gather the clusters of the vine of the earth, for the earth's grapes are fully ripe!" 19 The angel thrust his sickle into the earth, and gathered the vintage of the earth, and threw it into the great wine press of the wrath of God.

NLT Mt 24:48 But if the servant is evil and thinks, 'My master won't be back for a while,'

NLT Mt 24:49 and begins oppressing the other servants, partying, and getting drunk—

NLT Mt 24:50 well, the master will return unannounced and unexpected.

NLT Mt 24:51 He will tear the servant apart and banish him with the hypocrites. In that place there will be weeping and gnashing of teeth.

The servant who is evil, and is a Christian by profession only (not moved by the Lord's Spirit in them) will be assigned a place with the hypocrites. In reality, their profession of faith is hypocritical. That place where there will be weeping and gnashing of teeth is on earth during the time of the great tribulation. Those in the *Church Corrupt* are made pure through the great tribulation. This is why it says at the end of the testimony of the two witnesses:

NIV Rev 14:12 This calls for patient endurance on the part of the saints who obey God's commandments and remain faithful to Jesus.

NIV Rev 14:13 Then I heard a voice from heaven say, "Write: <u>Blessed are the dead who die in the Lord from now on." "Yes," says the Spirit, "they will rest from their labor, for their deeds will follow them."</u>

Blessed because in the days before the seventh trumpet sounds, they will also be caught up as the *Church Pure* had been.

NIV 1Th 4:13 Brothers, we do not want you to be ignorant about those who fall asleep (died), or to grieve like the rest of men, who have no hope.

NIV 1Th 4:14 We believe that Jesus died and rose again and so we believe that God will bring with Jesus those who have fallen asleep in him.

NIV 1Th 4:15 According to the Lord's own word, we tell you that we who are still alive, who are left till the coming of the Lord, will certainly not precede those who have fallen asleep.

NIV 1Th 4:16 For the Lord himself will come down from heaven, with a loud command, with the voice of the archangel and with the trumpet call of God, and the dead in Christ will rise first.

NIV 1Th 4:17 After that, we who are still alive and are left will be caught up together with them in the clouds to meet the Lord in the air. And so we will be with the Lord forever.

Those who died in the great tribulation and were faithful to their testimony will rise from the dead as the two witnesses had. Those who are in *spiritual union* with Christ have no need to be resurrected. When they die to their physical bodies, even before their heads hit the ground in death, they are alive before God in heaven. They find themselves clothed in a celestial body, never having experienced death in any form. Likewise, those who are caught up as the *Church Pure* are not in need of a resurrection either because at the rapture they receive their celestial bodies without even as much as tasting death. Only those who were true to the testimony of Christ and die during the great tribulation will have need to be resurrected at the first resurrection. Those who survive and are faithful to their testimony, together with those who rose from the dead, will be given a celestial body, and lifted up to meet Jesus in the sky joining the *Church Pure*. This event is called the first resurrection.

NIV Rev 20:4 I saw thrones on which were seated those who had been given authority to judge.

Those seated on the thrones are the *Church Pure*, the wheat who went to the Lord before the grapes. Then below the *Church Corrupt* who had been refined by the great tribulation joins them:

NIV Rev 20:4 . . . *And I saw the souls of those who had been beheaded because of their testimony for Jesus and because of the word of God. They had not worshiped the beast or his image and had not received his mark on their foreheads or their hands. They came to life and reigned with Christ a thousand years.*

NIV Rev 20:5 *(The rest of the dead did not come to life until the thousand years were ended.)* *This is the first resurrection.*

NIV Rev 20:6 *Blessed and holy are those who have part in the first resurrection.* The second death has no power over them, but they will be priests of God and of Christ and will reign with him for a thousand years.

Jesus had warned the Church of their grave condition in the letters to the seven Churches.

NIV Rev 3:15 These are the words of the Amen, the faithful and true witness, the ruler of God's creation.

NIV Rev 3:15 I know your deeds, that you are neither cold nor hot. I wish you were either one or the other!

NIV Rev 3:16 *So, because you are lukewarm—neither hot nor cold—I am about to spit you out of my mouth.*

NIV Rev 3:17 You say, 'I am rich; I have acquired wealth and do not need a thing.' But you do not realize that you are wretched, pitiful, poor, blind and naked.

NIV Rev 3:18 *I counsel you to buy from me gold refined in the fire, so you can become rich; and white clothes to wear,* so you can cover your shameful nakedness; and salve to put on your eyes, so you can see.

That gold refined in the fire that Jesus speaks of is the great tribulation. After He has divorced the *Church Corrupt* (spit them out of His mouth) they are on their own. However, all hope is not lost, just as with Hosea's wife Gomer, if they do as the two witnesses instructed, they will become as gold refined in the fire. They will be received by the Lord once again. That is if they follow the Lord's counsel after He leaves them to the time of judgment.

NIV Rev 3:19 Those whom I love I rebuke and discipline. So be earnest, and repent.

NIV Rev 3:20 Here I am! I stand at the door and knock. If anyone hears my voice and opens the door, I will come in and eat with him, and he with me.

NIV Rev 3:21 To him who overcomes, I will give the right to sit with me on my throne, just as I overcame and sat down with my Father on his throne.

NIV Rev 3:22 He who has an ear, let him hear what the Spirit says to the churches."

Jesus warns us in Matthew just as He did in the seven letters:

NLT Mt 25:24 . . . "Then the servant with the one bag of gold came and said, 'Sir, I know you are a hard man, harvesting crops you didn't plant and gathering crops you didn't cultivate.

NLT Mt 25:25 I was afraid I would lose your money, so I hid it in the earth and here it is.'

NLT Mt 25:26 "But the master replied, 'You wicked and lazy servant! You think I'm a hard man, do you, harvesting crops I didn't plant and gathering crops I didn't cultivate?

NLT Mt 25:27 Well, you should at least have put my money into the bank so I could have some interest.

NLT Mt 25:28 Take the money (My Holy Spirit) from this servant and give it to the one with the ten bags of gold.

NLT Mt 25:29 To those who use well what they are given, even more will be given, and they will have an abundance. But from those who are unfaithful, even what little they have will be taken away.

NLT Mt 25:30 Now throw this useless servant into outer darkness, where there will be weeping and gnashing of teeth (the great tribulation).'

It is important to recognize, however, that it is not just by enduring the great tribulation that will purify them, but to endure the great tribulation as the two witnesses instructed and demonstrated for them to do. That is, to not come off their testimony (their profession of faith), do not worship the beast, and do not take his mark, even under the penalty of death. In this way their profession is made true.

WEB Rev 14:20 The wine press was trodden outside of the city, and blood came out of the wine press, even to the bridles of the horses, as far as one thousand six hundred stadia.

The grapes are the *Church Corrupt*. Being crushed and trodden in the wine press is the time of the great tribulation. The blood that comes out of the grapes when trodden is the blood of the Christians who are killed in the great tribulation. The height to a horses bridle is about four to six feet. One thousand six hundred stadia, is approximately 200 miles. This is saying that there is enough blood spilled during the great tribulation that if it were all together it could form a river 5 feet deep for 200 miles. The average human at 150 pounds holds about 5-1/2 quarts of blood in their body. John told us that those who gain their celestial bodies by dying in the great tribulation were so numerous that he calls them, "a great multitude that no one could count."

NIV Rev 7:9 After this I looked and there before me was a great multitude that no one could count, from every nation, tribe, people and language, standing before the throne and in front of the Lamb. They were wearing white robes and were holding palm branches in their hands.

NIV Rev 7:10 And they cried out in a loud voice: "Salvation belongs to our God, who sits on the throne, and to the Lamb."

NIV Rev 7:11 All the angels were standing around the throne and around the elders and the four living creatures. They fell down on their faces before the throne and worshiped God,

NIV Rev 7:12 saying: "Amen! Praise and glory and wisdom and thanks and honor and power and strength be to our God for ever and ever. Amen!"

NIV Rev 7:13 Then one of the elders asked me, "These in white robes—who are they, and where did they come from?"

NIV Rev 7:14 I answered, "Sir, you know." And he said, "These are they who have come out of the great tribulation (the grapes); they have washed their robes and made them white in the blood of the Lamb.

Rev 7:15 Therefore, "they are before the throne of God and serve him day and night in his temple; and he who sits on the throne will spread his tent over them.

NIV Rev 7:16 Never again will they hunger; never again will they thirst. The sun will not beat upon them, nor any scorching heat.

NIV Rev 7:17 For the Lamb at the center of the throne will be their shepherd; he will lead them to springs of living water. And God will wipe away every tear from their eyes."

CHAPTER 8

The Seven Angels with the Seven Bowls of Wrath

Seven Angels with Seven Plagues

WEB Rev 15:1 I saw another great and marvelous sign in the sky: seven angels having the seven last plagues, for in them God's wrath is finished.

Peter said:

NIV 1Pe 4:16 However, if you suffer as a Christian, do not be ashamed, but praise God that you bear that name.
NIV 1Pe 4:17 For it is time for judgment to begin with the family of God; and if it begins with us, what will the outcome be for those who do not obey the gospel of God?
NIV 1Pe 4:18 And, "If it is hard for the righteous to be saved, what will become of the ungodly and the sinner?"
NIV 1Pe 4:19 So then, those who suffer according to God's will should commit themselves to their faithful Creator and continue to do good.

The great tribulation has run its course of 3-1/2 years. The Church had become empowered by prostituting herself to Babylon, then finally she became the seventh kingdom of Babylon; in order to keep Babylon (her power base) from perishing. If the Lord is to utterly and perfectly destroy every trace of Babylon for it never to rise from its ashes, then He must be just as thorough destroying it in the Church as He is at destroying it in the world.

NIV Rev 17:15 *Then the angel said to me, "The waters you saw, where the prostitute sits, are peoples, multitudes, nations and languages.*
NIV Rev 17:16 *The beast and the ten horns you saw will hate the prostitute. They will bring her to ruin and leave her naked; they will eat her flesh and burn her with fire.*
NIV Rev 17:17 *For God has put it into their hearts to accomplish his purpose by agreeing to give the beast their power to rule, until God's words are fulfilled.*
NIV Rev 17:18 *The woman you saw is the great city that rules over the kings of the earth."*

That was always the purpose of the great tribulation—to purify and destroy Babylon in the Church. It is the only reason the Lord had granted evil the power to dominate the world. In addition, the world has forever required that they live under the line of offspring of the Devil and his antichrist. The world has from the beginning up to this day and until Nimrod returns from the dead; prays, fasts, strives for, and has been bent on being ruled by Babylon and its founder. In doing so, the world therefore is demonstrating their defiance and rebellion towards the true God.

The pursuit of this rebellion is done through the mythologies of the world, religious practices of the world, even in an overwhelming amount of the practices within the Christian Church are Babylonian in origin. Like, for example, Easter and Christmas traditions. When it comes to the Church, in large part, it is practiced in ignorance as well as in a spirit of deaf and dumbness. That is a numbness which blinds the people and deceives them of the significance of their traditions and practices.

However, this does not make it innocent or insignificant. The Lord spoke to Ezekiel in regards to this very indifferent attitude when it comes to the practices and traditions of Easter. Easter is a Babylonian holiday which celebrates Ishtar and Nimrod coming back from the dead, and beckons him to return again. This holiday/worship was established thousands of years before Christ was born.

NIV Eze 8:12 He said to me, "Son of man, have you seen what the elders of the house of Israel are doing in the darkness, each at the shrine of his own idol? They say, 'The LORD does not see us; the LORD has forsaken the land.'"

NIV Eze 8:13 Again, he (the Lord) said, "You will see them doing things that are even more detestable."

NIV Eze 8:14 Then he brought me to the entrance to the north gate of the house of the LORD, <u>and I saw women sitting there, mourning Tammuz.</u>

This mourning was done for 40 days and is the origin of the 40 day fast of lent that the Church practices. Tammuz was worshiped as the risen Nimrod. In reality, Tammuz was the son of Nimrod born after he had died. He was worshiped as the risen Nimrod and as such, his mother Ishtar (who "Easter" is named after) married him and remained the queen of Babylon.

NIV Eze 8:15 He said to me, "Do you see this, son of man? You will see things that are even more detestable than this."

NIV Eze 8:16 He then brought me into the inner court of the house of the LORD, and there at the entrance to the temple, between the portico and the altar, were about twenty-five men. <u>With their backs toward the temple of the LORD and their faces toward the east, they were bowing down to the sun in the east.</u>

This is the origin of the tradition of holding the Easter sunrise service. It was originally practiced because Nimrod is the sun god and originator of sun worship.

NIV Eze 8:17 He said to me, "Have you seen this, son of man? <u>Is it a trivial matter for the house of Judah to do the detestable things they are doing here?</u> Must they also fill the land with violence and continually provoke me to anger? Look at them putting the branch to their nose (this is to giving an obscene gesture—they are openly defying the Lord and He is insulted)!

NIV Eze 8:18 Therefore I will deal with them in anger; I will not look on them with pity or spare them. Although they shout in my ears, I will not listen to them."

To be purged of this spiritual adultery and to wake up from its spell, it will require the great tribulation for many Christians. However, in this part of the narrative, the great tribulation has occurred, Babylon in the Church has been purged. Now it is the time for Babylon in the world, who rules the entire globe, to be utterly destroyed, never again to rise up from its ashes. This prophetic profile reflects a "sevenness" to the punishment and destruction of Babylon in the world. That means there will be administered a perfect and totally complete wrath and punishment from God.

For the Christians, we learned in the seven letters to the seven churches that the great tribulation has a tenness to it. The difference between tenness and the sevenness when it comes to God's wrath is as the difference between discipline and punishment. Although painful, when discipline is complete it causes the one under it to be closer to God than ever before—even reconciled. Whereas punishment drives one away from God into the darkness where one is destroyed. That is exactly what has happened (below) concerning those Christians who died holding fast to their testimony in Christ having been disciplined in the great tribulation.

> WEB Rev 15:2 *I saw something like a sea of glass mixed with fire, and those who overcame the beast, his image, and the number of his name, standing on the sea of glass, having harps of God.*

These who "overcame the beast" during the great tribulation but died hanging true to their testimony in Christ, are in the paradisiacal realm of Hades. The last verse of the prophetic picture which precedes this one was telling us about how these who overcame the beast had been purified as grapes in a wine press, and their blood ran like a river 200 miles long.

The first couple verses in this prophetic profile tell us by inference that the great tribulation is finished, the wrath of God against Babylon in the world has begun, and the martyred in Christ watch on as God executes His justice. This was a justice He had promised to those martyred under the altar but was delayed until the full number of them was complete. With those who are martyred in the great tribulation the full number has finally become complete.

Now the martyred watch on as the judgment of fire comes down upon their enemies. They are now observing through a portal of sorts what is going on in the world they are no longer in. That portal is described here as like a sea of glass they can stand on and look down at the world seeing it burn from the wrath of God against those who killed them.

WEB Rev 15:3 *They sang the song of Moses, the servant of God, and the song of the Lamb, saying, "Great and marvelous are your works, Lord God, the Almighty! Righteous and true are your ways, you King of the nations. ⁴ᵃ Who wouldn't fear you, Lord, and glorify your name? For you only are holy.*

They sing and celebrate the Lord's justice against them. However, most importantly, they celebrate the greatness of God which was able to save them even from death, and marvel at His power.

NLT Rev 14:12 *Let this encourage God's holy people to endure persecution patiently and remain firm to the end, obeying his commands and trusting in Jesus."*
NLT Rev 14:13 *And I heard a voice from heaven saying, "Write this down: <u>Blessed are those who die in the Lord from now on. Yes, says the Spirit, they are blessed indeed, for they will rest from all their toils and trials; for their good deeds follow them!"</u>*

It turns out just as the two witnesses told them (above) it would, and as they had demonstrated with their own lives. Though they were left behind to endure the great tribulation, they had the courage to follow the admonishment from Jesus in the letter to the church in Laodicea, as well as the warnings of the two witnesses. They were not let down, indeed they became blessed.

There is another place in Revelation that we hear about a "sea of glass".

NIV Rev 4:2 *At once I was in the Spirit, and there before me was a throne in heaven with someone sitting on it.*
NIV Rev 4:3 *And the one who sat there had the appearance of jasper and carnelian. A rainbow, resembling an emerald, encircled the throne.*
NIV Rev 4:4 *Surrounding the throne were twenty-four other thrones, and seated on them were twenty-four elders. They were dressed in white and had crowns of gold on their heads.*
NIV Rev 4:5 *From the throne came flashes of lightning, rumblings and peals of thunder. Before the throne, seven lamps were blazing. These are the seven spirits of God.*
NIV Rev 4:6 *<u>Also before the throne there was what looked like a sea of glass, clear as crystal.</u> In the center, around the throne, were four living creatures, and they were covered with eyes, in front and in back.*

From their thrones the Father, and the Son, and the 24 elders observe what is happening in the world through the sea of glass. On this occasion there is no fire mixed in the sea of glass because the seven years of wrath God pours out has not started.

> WEB Rev 15:4b For all the nations will come and worship before you. For your righteous acts have been revealed."

Their prophetic song of praise prophesize the results after all is said and done and Jesus has returned to rule the earth. The victory will be the Lord's and He will show the greatness of both His power and His mercy. Nevertheless, at this moment it is before the first resurrection of the dead. Those who have died are disembodied in the paradisiacal place of Hades and are out of reach of all the violence and hatred projected towards them.

Those Christians who survived the great tribulation now have a mark from God on their forehead and cannot be harmed, not by the world who wants them dead, and not by the plagues which will now befall the earth. In the days before the seventh trumpet sounds, those who died while holding fast to their testimony in Christ during the great tribulation, will once again be clothed with a body and rise from the dead. Then sometime after the dead in Christ rise in the first resurrection, both them and the ones who survived (but did not become untrue to their testimony or take the mark of the beast or worship him) will together rise in the sky and line up behind Jesus who is poised to return to the earth.

All of the earth will see Jesus in the sky above them collecting His bride, His celestial humans who will come back with Him and rule the whole earth. However, while the whole earth sees above their heads from horizon to horizon Jesus in the sky ready to return along with His host who they had betrayed and killed, the seven bowls of God's wrath will be poured out on them. It is like the navy pummeling with artillery fire and the air force with bombs every square inch of an island for days before the marines land on the beach and take the island.

First there is a trumpet blast that the earth will hear, then from the heavens an angel with a bowl filled with a plague will be poured out on the inhabitants of the earth.

Note: Despite the fact that the seven trumpets and the seven bowls do not seem to match each other (the first trumpet lining up with the first bowl, and so on) they actually do if you understand how they correlate to each other, and why they were put in that particular order.

All the while these plagues are being poured out or administered, Jesus and His host are literally visible from horizon to horizon for eight out of every 24 hours. This is possibly due to a tear in the sky which rolls back. It opens the sky to this spectacle in the spiritual realm. He is poised to come back to take rule of the earth. When the seventh trumpet sounds He will have returned and will have the final battle which will give Jesus authority over the entire globe—Armageddon.

> WEB Rev 15:5 *After these things I looked, and the temple of the tabernacle of the testimony in heaven was opened. 6The seven angels who had the seven plagues came out, clothed with pure, bright linen, and wearing golden sashes around their breasts. 7 One of the four living creatures gave to the seven angels seven golden bowls full of the wrath of God, who lives forever and ever. 8 The temple was filled with smoke from the glory of God, and from his power. No one was able to enter into the temple, until the seven plagues of the seven angels would be finished.*

". . . the temple of the tabernacle of the testimony in heaven was opened. The seven angels who had the seven plagues came out. . . " At the beginning of the story of the fall of man we were told something similar happened in the temple of God in heaven.

Amp Rev 11:19 Then the sanctuary of God in heaven was thrown open, and the ark of His covenant was seen standing inside in His sanctuary

We have been describing the response of God towards the original sin as His judgment and redemption. We have also discovered that the scroll with seven seals held God's plan of judgment and redemption.

When God reacted in His temple with lightnings, thunders, hail, and earthquakes at that fateful moment when Eve and the Devil sinned, the ark of the covenant was revealed. That ark was our Savior and Lord, the child of Eve, and the First Born of many brethrens. In Him being revealed while embodying the promises and salvation of God, He was/is God's redemption which was visible in the temple in heaven.

Now, as His plans come to a close, in this part of the narrative, we see something else in the heavenly temple of God. That is, as it says above, the seven angels who have seven bowls of plagues to pour out onto the world. It is His judgment that has been revealed when His temple opens up this time. Concerning both redemption and judgment we can understand and believe very clearly they are from God Himself. For both are represented as coming out of the temple where God the Father resides, then executed both His judgment and redemption in the world.

In the first narrative, which was about the opening of the seven seals, when the seventh seal had been opened it released seven trumpet blasts. Each of those trumpet blasts released a portion or a seventh of God's wrath on Babylon in the world. Together, these seven trumpet blasts represent the sevenness of God's wrath and punishment against Babylon in the world. Babylon in the world is the empire and ruler of the line of offspring of the Devil.

A description of that perfect and complete outpouring of God's wrath is repeated in this second narrative in order for this narrative to be complete in its composition. The outpouring of the seven bowls of God's wrath is not something different from the seven trumpet blasts, but the same event told in a different story/narrative.

Note: The first narrative, which is *Volume 3, The Seven Seals of Revelation,* covers the trumpets and bowls in much greater detail in chapter 8, than here in *Volume 4.* The authors recommend referring to *Volume 3,* chapter 8 if more detailed coverage is needed.

As typical in Revelation, this instance which tells of the same event uses different wording as the other occasion. Likewise, it tells us of different particulars about the event as the previous narrative. In this way, we can get more information on the same subject. Secondly, as visions do, spreading out the information in different books or narratives using different wording and describing different particulars encrypts the message.

Amp Da 12:1 And at that time [of the end] Michael shall arise, the great [angelic] prince who defends and has charge of your [Daniel's] people. And there shall be a time of trouble, straitness, and distress such as never was since there was a nation till that time. But at that time your people shall be delivered, everyone whose name shall be found written in the Book [of God's plan for His own].

Amp Da 12:2 And many of those who sleep in the dust of the earth shall awake: some to everlasting life and some to shame and everlasting contempt and abhorrence.

Amp Da 12:3 And the teachers and those who are wise shall shine like the brightness of the firmament, and those who turn many to righteousness (to uprightness and right standing with God) [shall give forth light] like the stars forever and ever.

Amp Da 12:4 But you, O Daniel, shut up the words and seal the Book until the time of the end. [Then] many shall run to and fro and search anxiously [through the Book], and knowledge [of God's purposes as revealed by His prophets] shall be increased and become great.

Finally, Revelation and prophecy in general is composed by God this way in the Bible because it forces the readers to show some diligence and fortitude in desiring to know the truth. By requiring the student to carefully go "to and fro" through the Scriptures in order to put it all together and know the subject. This kind of diligence reveals the individual's willingness and determination to know the truth. This way the sincere will have to dig a bit in order to find the full meaning, demonstrating to God their true heart. In turn, the Lord will release His Spirit giving interpretation to those of His choosing.

The Seven Bowls of God's Wrath

WEB Rev 16:1 I heard a loud voice out of the temple, saying to the seven angels, "Go and pour out the seven bowls of the wrath of God on the earth!"

Now begins the punishment of Babylon in the world! The Lord becomes active in the earth again after a 3-1/2 year global desolation. He brings the great tribulation to a grinding halt by giving the surviving Christians a mark which protects them, and by punishing plagues which shift the focus of the world from killing believers to their own survival.

WEB Rev 16:2 **The first** went, and poured out his bowl into the earth, and it became a harmful and evil sore on the people who had the mark of the beast, and who worshiped his image. [3] **The second angel** poured out his bowl into the sea, and it became blood as of a dead man. Every living thing in the sea died. [4] **The third** poured out his bowl into the rivers and springs of water, and they became blood. [5] I heard the angel of the waters saying, "You are righteous, who are and who were, you Holy One, because you have judged these things. [6] For they poured out the blood of the saints and prophets, and you have given them blood to drink. They deserve this." [7] I heard the altar saying, "Yes, Lord God, the Almighty, true and righteous are your judgments." [8] **The fourth** poured out his bowl on the sun, and it was given to him to scorch men with fire. [9] People were scorched with great heat, and people blasphemed the name of God who has the power over these plagues. They didn't repent and give him glory. [10] **The fifth** poured out his bowl on the throne of the beast, and his kingdom was darkened. They gnawed their tongues because of the pain, [11] and they blasphemed the God of heaven because of their pains and their sores. They didn't repent of their works.

The first five trumpet blasts and bowls of wrath are released simultaneously much in the same way that the first four seals are released simultaneously. Both the seven trumpets/bowls can be categorized into two different types of punishment. The first category is natural disasters, "acts of God" as the insurance industry refers to them. God uses nature and His plans to lift the earth into the spiritual realm out of the natural universe as a means to punish the inhabitants of the earth.

Amp Rev 8:13 Then I [looked and I] saw a solitary eagle flying in midheaven, and as it flew I heard it crying with a loud voice, <u>Woe, woe, woe to those who dwell on the earth, because of the rest of the trumpet blasts</u> (bowls) <u>which the three angels are about to sound!</u>

The last three trumpets/bowls are far more severe and fall into a different type of category. They are not earthquakes, hail, darkness, or the sky tearing open, but the supernatural invading the natural. These last three plagues are most definitely more lethal and terrifying than natural disasters. When warning of them the angel says "Woe, woe woe . . . " they are three woes and the angel is making it clear that all three are a woe unto themselves, as the underlined part of verse 13 shows us above. They are living creatures of the supernatural who torment, kill, and defeat the armies of the earth.

These three woes happen one after another spanning the entire 3-1/2 years of punishment. There are four natural disasters that are released the moment this time period begins and the great tribulation ends. Along with the release of those four natural disasters one woe is released with them. Then later the second woe or the sixth trumpet and sixth bowl are executed. Finally, after the seventh trumpet sounds the last bowl is executed.

The opening of the sixth seal describes well what befalls earth suddenly. The very minute the last person killed that brings the dead in Christ to the full, life on earth will change.

The Sixth Seal—Terror

NAS REV 6:12 *I looked when He broke the sixth seal, and there was a great earthquake; and the sun became black as sackcloth made of hair, and the whole moon became like blood;*
NAS REV 6:13 *and the stars of the sky fell to the earth, as a fig tree casts its unripe figs when shaken by a great wind.*

The above two verses describe the first 3-1/2 years which are the great tribulation and are pointed towards the Christians. The earthquake happens at the rapture collapsing a tenth of Jerusalem while killing seven thousand people. Then the great tribulation begins with the stars falling from the sky to the earth as unripen figs fall from a fig tree in high winds. Those stars are the Christians who are killed by the winds of destruction.

The below verses describe what suddenly happens to the people of the earth the moment the great tribulation is brought to an end. What is described is the first five trumpet blasts and their corresponding bowls of God's wrath.

NAS REV 6:14 *The sky was split apart like a scroll when it is rolled up, and every mountain and island were moved out of their places.*
NAS REV 6:15 *Then the kings of the earth and the great men and the commanders and the rich and the strong and every slave and free man hid themselves in the caves and among the rocks of the mountains;*
NAS REV 6:16 *and they said to the mountains and to the rocks, "Fall on us and hide us from the presence of Him who sits on the throne, and from the wrath of the Lamb;*
NAS REV 6:17 *for the great day of their wrath has come, and who is able to stand?"*

Here is a synopsis of what happens on the first day the great tribulation ends:

The first thing that happens is that the accuser of the brethren, Satan (also called the Devil), is subdued. He is not only expelled from God's presence where he stood as prosecutor seeking the death penalty against every believer, but is expelled from the heavens or the spiritual realm. Notwithstanding that he is a celestial creature, he is cast down to the earth. This is a literal happening! The world will see the form of the Devil and he and other supernatural creatures will interact with natural humans (Rev 12:14-17). Heaven or the spiritual realm is cleaned up first and all the fallen angels who followed the Devil are cast down to the earth with him. This single act stops the killing of the Christians because God's leave to kill and persecute the Christians has ended; He will not hear another case against them. Thus the expulsion from heaven of the Devil, the accuser of the brethren.

The Devil, in his descent to the earth, is in a rage because of this development. Since the Christians are either raptured out of reach in heaven, or have a mark which takes any authority away from him to harm, he decides to spend his rage on the Jews. However, God gives them a place to hide away from him (Rev 12:14).

On his way out of heaven he is given the key to the Abyss (Rev 9:1-12). The Abyss, also referred to as the bottomless pit, is a place of special reserve in Hades, the realm of the dead. It is like the solitary confinement with the highest security inside a prison. The Abyss is meant to confine the fallen angels who took natural women as wives. Also for their offspring the giants/Nephilim and every other abortion of nature caused by the manipulation of genetics, perverting them in ways which lead up to the flood. These genetically altered creatures died in the flood and have been confined to the Abyss, along with all the evil and ungodly celestial creatures who possess spiritual bodies that God has been protecting the earth from. However, when the Devil is thrown down to the earth and is manifest, the corrupt angels who followed him are also thrown down at the same time, along with these celestial creatures who the Devil lets free out of the Abyss.

NIV Rev 9:7 The locusts looked like horses prepared for battle. On their heads they wore something like crowns of gold, and their faces resembled human faces.
NIV Rev 9:8 Their hair was like women's hair, and their teeth were like lions' teeth.

NIV Rev 9:9 *They had breastplates like breastplates of iron, and the sound of their wings was like the thundering of many horses and chariots rushing into battle.*

NIV Rev 9:10 *They had tails and stings like scorpions, and in their tails they had power to torment people for five months.*

These hordes of locust like creatures, who come out of the Abyss and sting like scorpions, circle the globe. Their sting will not kill but issue pain like a scorpion bite only more severely and lasting five months. Between the Devil, the fallen angels, and ungodly creatures streaming out of the Abyss in such quantity, they block out the sky. Thus as it says (Rev. 9:2), that the sun will grow dark being blotted out as by smoke because of the stream of these supernatural creatures, known as the first woe, coming out from the Abyss. It will be like our worst nightmares have become reality. Only those who know and understand the book of Revelation will know this is not the end of life and that it will last only for 3-1/2 years. This prophetic knowledge will be their hope.

To make it possible for the natural to interact with the supernatural, God suddenly moves the earth dimensionally. There is a tear in the fabric of space and time and the earth starts slipping through it into the spiritual realm. At first, it only crowns into the spiritual realm. This crowning upsets the rotation of the earth in that there is no longer 12 hours of the day sky with the sun. Likewise, no longer are there 12 hours of the night sky with the moon and planets reflecting the sun and the light of the stars. Instead there are only 8 hours of the day sky, then 8 hours of the night sky. Then from horizon to horizon there is a view of the spiritual realm for 8 hours. Eventually the entire earth slips into the spiritual realm, and is no longer part of the natural universe.

However, there are no planets, stars, suns, or moons in the spiritual realm. There is no source of light for the earth when it finishes its shift into the next dimension. This tear in the fabric of space and time is so violent that it somewhat "accordions up" space to open up the tear so the earth can pass through. In doing so, it shakes all the heavenly bodies in the natural universe. Another effect is that the scrunching or "accordioning up" of space puts the earth closer to the sun. This causes unbearable heat, burning of the skin, and causes spontaneous fires to break out. In addition, fresh water sources dry up due to the scorching heat of the sun. It burns up the vegetation and destroys the landscape. In this process of the earth pushing through from one dimension to another it's shape gets distorted just as a baby's head when passing through the birth canal. This causes violent earthquakes, horrific and devastating tsunamis' like the world has never known. Ones which wash away islands. There are tectonic plate movements which cause severe earthquakes, and mountains to be leveled. The whole topography of the earth changes. During the 8 hour view of the sky which faces the spiritual realm, there would be only darkness except for one thing. That is the promised sign of the return of the Son of Man, the most spectacular phenomena ever in the history of the natural universe:

NIV Mt 24:29 *"Immediately after the distress of those days " 'the sun will be darkened, and the moon will not give its light; the stars will fall from the sky, and the heavenly bodies will be shaken.'*

Above, Jesus is describing the process of the earth moving into the spiritual realm from the natural universe. It is immediately after the great tribulation.

NIV Mt 24:30 *"<u>At that time the sign of the Son of Man will appear in the sky, and all the nations of the earth will mourn.</u> They will see the Son of Man coming on the clouds of the sky, with power and great glory.*
NIV Mt 24:31 *And he will send his angels with a loud trumpet call, and they will gather his elect from the four winds, from one end of the heavens to the other.*

The sign of the Son of Man returning in the sky from horizon to horizon for 8 hours every day will be an amazing and hopeful sight to some, but a terrifying and undoing sight to others. People will look and see up in the sky, Jesus poised to return to the earth. However, before He actually comes down in the days before the seventh trumpet blast, the millions, even hundreds of millions, of those killed in the great tribulation will rise from the dead in the first resurrection; once again terrifying the people of the world who killed them. Together, the living with a mark of God on their heads and the risen dead, will go up into the sky and line up behind Jesus alongside the celestial humans who are already with Him. That includes those who were raptured before the great tribulation.

The sign of the Son of Man in the sky for 8 hours every day will only last until Jesus comes down to the earth. About that time, however, the earth is completely pushed into the spiritual realm. When that happens, the earth will have no heavenly lights to be illuminated with. It will have been plunged into total darkness. That is, not the kind of darkness we have during the night when the stars and the moon are out, but utter darkness so thick you cannot see your own hand in front of you.

The fabric of space and time tear and the sign of the Son of Man is seen in the sky. Devastating and terrifying acts of nature distress the earth as a result of the happenings on the first day of God's wrath being poured out. However, the effects of these events start with a measured portion (1/3) then before they are done, they consume in their entirety. For example, 8 hours of the day and night sky are lost to the spiritual realm, then eventually the earth is plunged into total darkness as it passes into the spirit realm. Just as right before the end and seventh bowl, the first resurrection will occur, terrifying the people even more. For them who do not understand, it is the night of the living dead—the dead they themselves killed.

Included with the plagues which happen simultaneously, are that the seas and the fresh water turn to blood. It will be just as in the days of Moses. It will first happen initially to 1/3 of the water sources but eventually spread to all of them. Ocean barring ships will be destroyed, as well as aquatic life, first 1/3 is damaged then eventually all.

With all these things suddenly destroying any and every semblance of life as it was known before this day, is it any wonder that rich and poor, strong and weak, ask the already crumbling mountains to fall on them and kill them? They do so in an effort to end the pain of the scorpion like creatures and hide them from the sight of the sign of the Son of Man coming.

NAS REV 6:14 *The sky was split apart like a scroll when it is rolled up, and every mountain and island were moved out of their places.*
NAS REV 6:15 *Then the kings of the earth and the great men and the commanders and the rich and the strong and every slave and free man hid themselves in the caves and among the rocks of the mountains;*

NAS REV 6:16 and they said to the mountains and to the rocks, "Fall on us and hide us from the presence of Him who sits on the throne, and from the wrath of the Lamb;

NAS REV 6:17 for the great day of their wrath has come, and who is able to stand?"

With four events of natural disasters there will be added the first woe consisting of the stinging scorpion like creatures. The first woe has passed.

*WEB Rev 16:12 **The sixth** poured out his bowl on the great river, the Euphrates. Its water was dried up, that the way might be prepared for the kings that come from the sunrise (the east).*

There is no way to tell how far into the 3-1/2 years the second woe comes. It could be 5 months after the first woe was released, or it could be 3 years after the wrath of God was released on the world. Nevertheless, this is the second woe. It is the release of a supernatural army of monsters from the spiritual realm. It is an army of 200,000,000, John tells us. This army circles the globe and kills off 1/3 of the world population.

In the prophetic profile of the Devil/red dragon, we are told:

NIV Rev 12:4 His tail swept a third of the stars out of the sky and flung them to the earth.

This is reference of the first 3-1/2 years during the great tribulation. Those stars swept away and flung to the earth is a prophetic picture of the Christians who will die in the great tribulation. Here we can know that 1/3 of the Christian population of the earth will be killed in the great tribulation.

In 2015 there were an estimated 2.3 billion Christians worldwide. At that time, there was a global population on earth of 7.3 billion people. That means that nearly 1/3 of the world's population is Christian. And a third of them will be killed. We are told that their spilled blood can form a 200 mile long river 4 to 6 feet deep. Some will have been raptured, 1/3 will die, and 2/3's of the Christians will survive and receive a mark on their head. That is, the ones who survive holding fast to their testimony of Christ, do not take the mark of the beast, or worship him. 1/3 of the Christian population in 2015 amounts to, 759,000,000 people. It already is 3 years later than 2015. Who knows how many Christians will be alive when the great tribulation comes.

It seems it is the justice of God that 1/3 are killed by this woe because the world will have killed 1/3 of the Christian population. As of 2015, there was an estimated 7.3 billion people on earth. If this army were to kill off 1/3 of the world population in 2015, they would circle the globe and kill 2,409,000,000 people worldwide. This does not include those who have the mark of God on their heads. Nor does this number include the Jews/Israelites who have a place of protection on the earth out of reach of all these plagues. For them this is not the first time, they were once before protected from all the plagues which befell Egypt. However, it has to be added to that huge number that are killed by this army from the spirit realm, all those who die from everything else that was going on in the earth; starvation, thirst, fires, natural disasters, people killing each other in an attempt to survive, and Lord knows what else.

Below is the account of the sixth bowl given in the previous narrative of the seven seals (*Volume 3*). In that account we have much greater detail that helps us understand what actually takes place. This Scripture (below) is the second woe as described after the sixth trumpet blast:

NIV Rev 9:14 It said to the sixth angel who had the trumpet, "Release the four angels who are bound at the great river Euphrates."

NIV Rev 9:15 And the four angels who had been kept ready for this very hour and day and month and year were released to kill a third of mankind.

NIV Rev 9:16 <u>*The number of the mounted troops was two hundred million. I heard their number.*</u>

NIV Rev 9:17 The horses and riders I saw in my vision looked like this: Their breastplates were fiery red, dark blue, and yellow as sulfur. The heads of the horses resembled the heads of lions, and out of their mouths came fire, smoke and sulfur.

NIV Rev 9:18 <u>*A third of mankind was killed by the three plagues of fire, smoke and sulfur that came out of their mouths.*</u>

NIV Rev 9:19 The power of the horses was in their mouths and in their tails; for their tails were like snakes, having heads with which they inflict injury.

NIV Rev 9:20 The rest of mankind that were not killed by these plagues still did not repent of the work of their hands; they did not stop worshiping demons, and idols of gold, silver, bronze, stone and wood—idols that cannot see or hear or walk.

NIV Rev 9:21 *Nor did they repent of their murders, their magic arts, their sexual immorality or their thefts.*

It's important to take note of the fact that even after all this, and knowing it is God who is punishing them, they do not repent. Below, in verses 16:13-16, we hear about what goes on after the second woe, and during the days right before the third and last woe.

> *WEB Rev 16:13* *I saw coming out of the mouth of the dragon, and out of the mouth of the beast, and out of the mouth of the false prophet, three unclean spirits, something like frogs;* <u>*14 for they are spirits of demons, performing signs; which go out to the kings of the whole inhabited earth, to gather them together for the war of that great day of God, the Almighty.*</u>

John was given a vision inside a vision by one of the elders of heaven to console him over no one being worthy of opening the scroll. In that vision, Jesus was pictured as a lamb with its throat cut, and having seven eyes and seven horns.

NIV Rev 5:6 *Then I saw a Lamb, looking as if it had been slain, standing in the center of the throne, encircled by the four living creatures and the elders.* <u>*He had seven horns and seven eyes, which are the seven spirits of God sent out into all the earth.*</u>

The seven horns are both the seven ages of the Church Age as well as the seven spirits of God which the eyes also represent. There is only one Holy Spirit, however, on several occasions He is spoken of as the seven spirits. In another place Jesus is said to hold in His hand the seven spirits.

NIV Rev 3:1 *... These are the words of* <u>*him who holds the seven spirits ...*</u>

Yet in another place we are told that the seven lampstands are the seven spirits of God:

NIV Rev 4:5 *... Before the throne,* <u>*seven lamps were blazing. These are the seven spirits of God*</u>

The Holy Spirit of God is being described as seven horns, seven eyes, seven lampstands, and something Jesus holds in His hand. In addition, the seven spirits, are the seven lampstands in verse 4:5 (above). However, in verse 1:20 (below) we are told the seven lampstands are the seven churches.

NIV Rev 1:20 *The mystery of the seven stars that you saw in my right hand and of the seven golden lampstands is this: The seven stars are the angels of the seven churches, <u>and the seven lampstands are the seven churches.</u>*

How do we reconcile all this? You could say the blazing fire in the seven lampstands is the Holy Spirit or the seven spirits of God. The seven lampstands actually embody the seven spirits (or the blazing flames). In that sense the embodiment of the Holy Spirit is the seven churches. That makes the seven churches the seven lampstands.

It says we were foreordained even before the creation of the world. The seven spirits within those seven lampstands are the fullness of the spirit of the bride of Christ. The spirit of the bride was already perfected even before the creation of the world. Those seven spirits are one—they are the Holy Spirit. The Holy Spirit is the Spirit of Christ which also is the Spirit of God. That is why the sacrificial lamb had seven eyes and seven horns. He had to die to His body so that His disembodied Spirit could be inhabited, even embodied by His people—His bride.

However, Jesus had not yet died before the creation of the world so that by His Spirit individual humans could become one flesh with Him, possessing His disembodied Spirit within them. That is the purpose of the seven lampstands which are ablaze with the seven spirits and are before the throne of heaven. Those lampstands embody the seven spirits of the bride before Jesus died for the Church—before they possess the Holy Spirit within them, His Spirit.

After Jesus died and during the seven ages of the Church those seven blazing spirits within the seven lampstands eventually go from being embodied by the lampstands, to being embodied by the individuals who comprise the Church throughout the seven Church ages. The individuals who comprise the Church are the temple of the Holy Spirit and they embody His Spirit. After the fullness of the seven spirits ablaze in the seven lampstands have come to reside and be embodied by the Church in their full numbers, those seven lampstands will no longer embody the seven spirits. Finally at that time, Jesus will have a face (or faces) to look at who embody the spirit of His bride. We are transformed and the spirit of His bride is embodied by us.

One final question: why seven spirits when the Holy Spirit is one, and is the Spirit of God? Because God is Spirit. The Holy Spirit is the part of Himself (if you will) which He has given to us to make us one with Him, as Jesus is one with Him. Seven, because just as there are seven heads or kingdoms or ages of the beast, there are seven ages to the Church Age. The difference being there is only one head, Christ, unlike the seven heads of the beast even if there are seven ages of the Church Age, which by the power granted them have seven different characteristics.

Jesus spoke the words of His testimony back when He walked the earth. He said of them that His words were spirit. And that:

NIV Jn 6:63 The Spirit gives life; the flesh counts for nothing. <u>The words I have spoken to you are spirit and they are life</u>.
NIV Jn 6:64 Yet there are some of you who do not believe." For Jesus had known from the beginning which of them did not believe and who would betray him.
NIV Jn 6:65 He went on to say, "This is why I told you that no one can come to me unless the Father has enabled him."

Jesus went town to town and spoke the words His Father gave Him in the scroll to speak to us, and we heard them with our ears. The Father sends the seven spirits over the course of the seven church ages which enters our hearts, convicting us of our sin and witnessing that His words are truth. There is a power given the Holy Spirit to be present in every Church age. As a result, to this very day when we hear with our ears those words of Jesus spoken more than a thousand years ago, the seven spirits convict our hearts of sin and witness as truth those words we hear. It does so in the same power today as the day Jesus spoke them. Between the words and the Spirit which express a power in each Church age, to this day they can bring down to his knees the strongest man, even the most evil man. In this way, His words are Spirit.

How is this important to verses 16:13-14? It says the spirits of demons come out of the mouth of the Devil (dragon) who now is visible to the people of the earth, the beast and antichrist who had risen from the dead, and the false prophet who brought him back from the dead. The words which come out of the mouths of the Devil, the antichrist, and the false prophet (the pope) will be spirit too. However, it will be demonic spirits coming out of their mouths backing up their words, which are false to the truth. Nevertheless, as false as they are to the truth, they will be both powerful and compelling. Even overwhelming, with the most powerful emotions and passions generated by a skewed perception of reality. It will seem irresistible to not see things in the light they will present them. Like mob anger that takes over a crowd, it will be an overwhelming power to resist jumping on board, being moved by their demonic spirits.

We were informed that after the second woe, the world will not repent. Then we are told a couple of things before the third woe. To interject something between the woes and bowls that is not descriptive of the woes being revealed is unusual, or inconsistent from how things have been outlined. We are being told what will happen right before we are told what the third woe is.

We are first informed that the Devil, the antichrist, and the false prophet will be incredibly seductive in rallying the people of the earth into a battle against the Lord. Additionally, in the middle of John telling us this, Jesus interjects and speaks a word to the wise.

> NIV Rev 16:15 "Behold, I come like a thief! Blessed is he who stays awake and keeps his clothes with him, so that he may not go naked and be shamefully exposed."

By saying this here, Jesus is breaking in and interrupting the narrative, just as the heavenly elder interrupted the vision John was having that was so upsetting to him.

The point of Jesus doing so is that He desires to give us, even the world every chance. Why? Because this is the last chance! There is no walking away from this decision if one decides to follow the antichrist into this battle. To be on the wrong side of this fight will mean death to all who array against the Lord. Below in verse 16:16 we see exactly what battle this evil trio are seducing the world to join them in— Armageddon.

> WEB Rev 16:16 He gathered them together into the place which is called in Hebrew, Megiddo (Armageddon).

No one walks away from this battle. You show up, and your dead! Come even to see the spectacle and cheer the troops on, and your dead! Jesus says He will come like a thief. Actually, the people in the world will see Jesus up in the sky for 3-1/2 years poised to come down. In fact His descent will be seen by the entire world from the east to the west, they will see Him in the sky coming back. He will touch down after the first resurrection and the second catching up of His Church. As soon as His foot touches the ground at the Mount of Olives there will be a massive earthquake. His entire heavenly host will follow Him just as the city, the New Jerusalem, which comes down on its own hill. The Lord will remain behind the walls of that city for a time to enjoy His wedding feast. It is then that the people of the earth will be seduced into rising up against Him for the mother of all wars.

Perhaps what Jesus means by saying He comes like a thief, is that suddenly the world system will collapse, and just hours after that battle He will get down to the business of healing the earth, lifting the curses on it, and installing His just and merciful government.

"Blessed is he who stays awake and keeps his clothes with him, so that he may not go naked and be shamefully exposed." We natural humans are clothed with a body. Blessed are we if we stay awake, alert, and do not permit ourselves to be hypnotized and consequently fall under the evil spell of the antichrist, by showing up to oppose the Lord. If we make that mistake we will die. We will be naked, shamefully exposed as being a disembodied soul, incapable of participating in the world Jesus brings. Shamefully because all hope of a world which is healed is just hours away and it would pay to hang on just a little while longer.

After Jesus makes His plea for our own good, He says the antichrist rallies the world, gathering them to Armageddon to meet Jesus when He comes out from behind the walls of the New Jerusalem, in answer to their call to fight and resist Him. The pouring out of the seventh and final bowl is the third and last woe. When the bowl is poured out those who gathered die, everyone of them! This is why when it is poured out (below) a loud voice from the temple of heaven cries out, "It is done!"

The only ones who do not die are the Devil, the beast (antichrist) and the false prophet. All who gathered, go to Hades, the realm of the dead. The Devil is bound in chains and thrown into the Abyss (the bottomless pit) and will be freed from there to have one last showdown against the Lord. The beast, and the false prophet, will not die in that battle along with all they gathered to join them. It is impossible for them to do so. They instead "go on to their destruction." They both are thrown alive into the lake of fire experiencing their second death—the final and eternal death.

> WEB Rev 16:17 **The seventh** poured out his bowl into the air. A loud voice came out of the temple of heaven, from the throne, saying, "It is done!" [18] There were lightnings, sounds, and thunders; and there was a great earthquake, such as was not since there were men on the earth, so great an earthquake, so mighty. [19] The great city was divided into three parts, and the cities of the nations fell. <u>Babylon the great was remembered in the sight of God, to give to her the cup of the wine of the fierceness of his wrath.</u> [20] Every island fled away, and the mountains were not found. [21] Great hailstones, about the weight of a talent, came down out of the sky on people. People blasphemed God because of the plague of the hail, for this plague is exceedingly severe.

Bibliography

Amplified Bible. Scripture quotations marked (Amp) are taken from the Amplified Bible, Copyright © 1954, 1958, 1962, 1964, 1965, 1987 by The Lockman Foundation. Used by permission.

Hackett, C. &McClendon, D. (2015) *Christians remain world's largest religious group, but they are declining in Europe.* Retrieved April 2018, from Pew Research Center: http://www.pewresearch.org/fact-tank/2017/04/05/christians-remain-worlds-largest-religious-group-but-they-are-declining-in-europe/

New American Standard. Scripture quotations marked (NAS) are taken from the NEW AMERICAN STANDARD BIBLE®, Copyright © 1960,1962,1963,1968,1971,1972,1973,1975,1977,1995 by The Lockman Foundation. Used by permission.

New International Version. Scriptures taken from the Holy Bible, New International Version®, NIV®. Copyright © 1973, 1978, 1984 by Biblica, Inc.™ Used by permission of Zondervan. All rights reserved worldwide. www.zondervan.com The "NIV" and "New International Version" are trademarks registered in the United States Patent and Trademark Office by Biblica, Inc.™

New Living Translation. Holy Bible, New Living Translation copyright © 1996, 2004, 2007 by Tyndale House Foundation. Used by permission of Tyndale House Publishers Inc., Carol Stream, Illinois 60188. All rights reserved. New Living, NLT, and the New Living Translation logo are registered` trademarks of Tyndale House Publishers.

New Revised Standard Version Bible (NRSV), copyright © 1989 National Council of the Churches of Christ in the United States of America. Used by permission. All rights reserved worldwide.

Roman Catholic Ten Commandments. (2018, January 13). Retrieved April 2018, from The Ten Commandments: http://www.the-ten-commandments.org/romancatholic-tencommandments.html

The Message Bible. Scripture quotations marked MSG are taken from *THE MESSAGE*, copyright © 1993, 1994, 1995, 1996, 2000, 2001, 2002 by Eugene

ABOUT THE AUTHORS

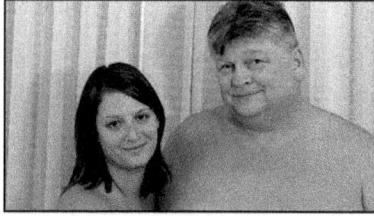

We are just a voice

WEB Jn 1:19 This is John's testimony (about himself), when the Jews sent priests and Levites from Jerusalem to ask him, "Who are you?"
WEB Jn 1:20 He declared, and didn't deny, but he declared, "I am not the Christ."
WEB Jn 1:21 They asked him, "What then? Are you Elijah?"
He said, "I am not."
"Are you the prophet?"
He answered, "No."
WEB Jn 1:22 They said therefore to him, "Who are you? Give us an answer to take back to those who sent us. What do you say about yourself?"
WEB Jn 1:23 He said, "__I am the voice__ of one crying in the wilderness, 'Make straight the way of the Lord . . ."

True prophets in the Bible did not convince people who they were; in fact, they refused to talk about themselves. They refused to bring credibility to the words of God they spoke by trying to get people to believe who they were and trust them. They knew that it would be profaning the words of God to do so, and it would be elevating themselves above God's words. They knew that God's words have their own credibility because they are from God. And God will show them (His own words) as from Him.

God's prophets also knew that those who truly love God will, therefore, benefit from their words, and those who are lovers of themselves will not benefit from them, because they will be dismissive and not trust them. The time is over that we look at the person who speaks to decide if we believe. We must begin to discern if the words are from God and if they carry God's Spirit.

You might say to that, "but not everyone can discern God." If that is the case, then they indict themselves as not being "known" by Jesus. They unwittingly reveal about themselves that they desire to do their own will and not the Lord's, just as the religious leaders who wanted Jesus to prove His credibility so they could decide if His words were from God.

Amp Jn 7:16 Jesus answered them by saying, My teaching is not My own, but His Who sent Me. Amp Jn 7:17 If any man desires to do His will (God's pleasure), he will know (have the needed illumination to recognize, and can tell for himself) whether the teaching is from God or whether I am speaking from Myself and of My own accord and on My own authority.

Many will think this is an oversimplified notion. However, it is so simple that it is not only true but reveals a simple but foundational truth about the person. What Jesus is saying is that if a man has a pure heart and wants to do the will of God above his own will, then what seems intuitively right (what sets well with that man) will be God's will and His words. However, even if you are a scholar, theologian, or work in the field of religion, and you desire to carry out your own will, having your own agendas and ambitions, well then, what seems right to that man is not God's will or His words, but that which lines up with his own will.

Generally speaking, the greatest religious minds in the world judge if something is from God by looking at the standing and qualifications of the man speaking them. In the above case, Jesus shows they may be smart in their own eyes, believing they know what is from God and therefore able to judge according to their knowledge of God. However, that would be saying in effect, we know everything about God because of our great knowledge. Therefore, if you say anything outside of our knowledge of God, or outside of the knowledge base of the accepted theological models, or if you are not a qualified student of those accepted models, then we must deduce your words are not from God.

To Jesus, they show about themselves that they don't recognize His words as from God because of their personal acquaintance with God. Instead, they have to judge by facts. They show themselves as having no real relationship with God; they would not recognize Him when He stands right before them. As a matter of fact, on another occasion when they showed contempt for Him, Jesus said of them:

NIV Jn 5:42 ... *but I know you. I know that you do not have the love of God in your hearts.*

They were once again wanting Him to prove who He was, and what right He had to talk the way He did. Jesus, instead of being intimidated, marveled at how He spoke and acted out everything the Father willed, yet they did not recognize His words as His Father's. Furthermore, they were, by nature, hostile and offended towards those words.

Let's look at that closer through an illustration. For example, you have a woman who claims to be married to a man named Jim. Then, a man claiming to be Jim and her husband approaches her. The above case is like the wife doubting this man is her husband. So then, she begins to question him. For example, "If you're Jim, when were you born?" And, "What kind of car did you have when you first got your license?" If he doesn't answer to her satisfaction, she decides that he is not her husband Jim. This might seem reasonable, and if he got the answers incorrect or didn't remember, the people listening might believe her when she says, "this is not my husband."

If there was anybody in the crowd that had wisdom, they might say this begs another question, "Hey lady, are you really Jim's wife or are you an imposter?" The reasoning of the wise man is, do you really need factual evidence to know if he is your husband? Don't you know your husband when he is standing right in front of you? Jesus is marveling at the religious leaders who are supposed to know God and claim to be in union with Him. However, they don't recognize Him when He stands before them. They don't even recognize His words as from God. Do they really need factual evidence to know something that they are supposed to have intimate knowledge of? Next question, why does it not occur to anyone to question if these men of God, leaders of the Jewish faith, may be imposters because they don't judge if someone and their words are from God by their intimate knowledge of God? They need factual evidence?

What did that tell Jesus? It told Him that even the top religious leaders who know the written word by heart can't recognize God when they stand right in front of Him.

It told Him that they were, in their inner man, hostile and threatened by God's words. It told Him that, in their inner selves, they really had no love or even any natural attraction towards God, His heart, and the Spirit of His words. They were obviously naturally repelled by them; they had no real love for God and their response showed it. However, to the religious leaders, they thought themselves wise and discerning to hold Jesus and His words suspect by judging Him with factual evidence. How disappointing it must have been to Jesus that the best of the best had no intimate knowledge of God and they were repulsed by Him when facing Him. Yes, Jesus' deduction was correct, there was no love of God in their hearts.

It is a Biblical fact that the major way we will be judged is it will be proven if we have a natural attraction to please God and do His will, therefore saying about us that we love Him more than ourselves. Learning by the folly of the leaders and the scholarly of Jesus' day, it is not by a knowledgeable and scholarly mind that one can successfully judge or discern what words coming from what person are from God or not. You can't judge superficially. No, it takes something much greater than to know every Bible verse by heart and to be able to have insightful knowledge of the person speaking them. It actually takes something much harder to attain than perfect scholarly knowledge of the written word. It takes a pure heart. Not meaning a sinless heart, but one which is single-minded, wanting to please God by serving Him and wanting to do His will at the expense of their own. This is what qualifies one to recognize if something is from God.

WEB Mt 5:8 Blessed are the pure in heart, for they shall see God.

It is true that as Colleen and I gain a larger following of our teachings and ministry, people will undoubtedly come to know us personally, and what kind of people we are. However, as teachers, we teach people how to live as spiritual men and women, discerning life in a spiritual way.

We have found the best way to teach discerning of spirit. It is not by knowing how to figure people out or to train them to have a spiritual power. No, we teach them to be single-minded when it comes to God, to be surrendered to His will in a pure or holistic way.

Having a still spirit which is not agitated with passions will create a huge contrast. The contrast of having the stillness of God's Spirit rule your heart coming in contact with the agitated spirit energies the people of this world operate out of makes one sensitive to discern spirit.

Jesus was right; wanting to do God's will with all your heart alone will cause you to recognize if one has God's Spirit in them and if they speak word's which are from God. As the saying goes, "You can't cheat an honest man."

NIV Jn 8:15 You judge by human standards. . .

NIV Jn 7:24 Stop judging by mere appearances, and make a right judgment."

As such, Colleen and I would like to be known first as a voice, just a voice. We want the words we speak from God to have more prominence and have their own credibility, than that of who we are. Therefore, we don't want to propagate people judging superficially if one is from God by giving our Bio. We want the words we speak to be more important than who we are. We want those who have a pure heart in wanting to serve God to check in their heart if we and the words we speak are from God.

We want those who don't have a pure heart to have a change of heart so they may know for themselves the voice and words of God when they hear them. However, we want to point people in the way to properly discern so they may know for themselves if we are from God and speak His words; in the same way John the Baptist tried to convey. You ask about us, and we will tell you about Him. You insist on wanting to know about us, and we will then tell you, we are just a voice making way for the One you should know and should be asking about. We are not a face or a name or people you should want to know, we are just a voice which gives voice to the One whose words you need to know.

OTHER BOOKS BY THE NAKED APOSTLES

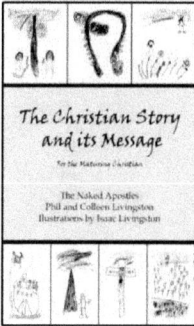

The Christian Story
and its Message

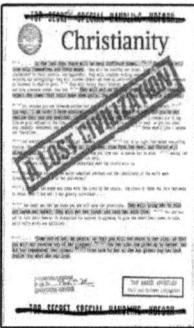

Christianity:
A Lost Civilization

For ordering information please visit our website at
www.nakedapostles.org

OTHER BOOKS BY THE NAKED APOSTLES

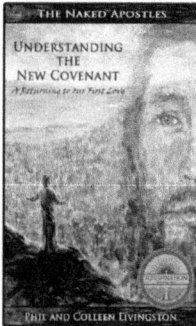

Understanding
the
New Covenant:
*A Returning to Our
First Love*

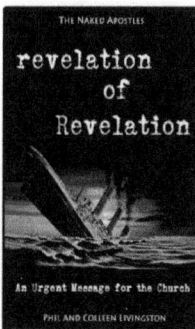

revelation of Revelation:
*An Urgent Message
for the Church*

Volumes 1-6

For ordering information please visit our website at
www.nakedapostles.org

www.ingramcontent.com/pod-product-compliance
Lightning Source LLC
LaVergne TN
LVHW051058080426
835508LV00019B/1952